SPANISH

IDIOMS, PROVERBS AND SLANG

OF

YESTERDAY AND TODAY

SPANISH

IDIOMS, PROVERBS AND SLANG

OF

YESTERDAY AND TODAY

JUAN SERRANO
SUSAN SERRANO

HIPPOCRENE BOOKS, INC.
New York

For information, address:
HIPPOCRENE BOOKS, INC.
171 Madison Avenue
New York, NY 10016

Cataloging-in-publication data available from the Library of Congress.

ISBN 0-7818-0675-5

Printed in the United States of America.

Contents

Introduction

✦✦✦

Spanish Idioms, Proverbs and Slang looks at the way Spanish folklore—the way of being and seeing the world—is reflected in language, and in particular in popular speech: the proverbs, idioms and slang expressions of yesteryear and today. It does this by analysing:

- the relationship between idioms, folk wisdom and popular humanism;
- the use of religious symbolism in modern colloquial Spanish, in particular in the mixture of religious and profane expressions which produce a language rich in colour, crude metaphor and picaresque wit;
- the use of the *vulgar* tongue in some of the classics of Spanish literature, as well as in lesser-known works, such as stories and satirical poems—some of which are still not available in translation, and therefore not easily accessible to the Anglo-Saxon world;
- the cross-current of influence between popular speech and literature;
- the *who, what, where, why and when* of many well-known Spanish sayings.

It is hoped that the book also reflects the desire of the early compilers of Spanish proverbs and idioms to bring together two seemingly opposing strains within both language and wisdom: the popular and the cultured aspects of language, and the homespun and scholarly wisdom.

The book is aimed at students of Spanish language and literature at all levels, as well as readers with a more general interest in Spanish studies. It presumes no knowledge of the language, and all Spanish terms are translated.

I

The People's Voice

"Proverbs . . . are like precious stones sprinkled on garments of great price, they captivate the eyes with their radiance, and their nature gives great pleasure to listeners and, being notable, they remain in the memory."[1]

—Mal Lara, *Phiosophia Vulgar*

The oral tradition as reflected in the language of proverbs, idioms and slang expressions is a manifestation of how and what *el vulgo*, ordinary people, believe, feel or think about the world in which they are immersed.

As in other languages, Spanish proverbs are mirrors of the popular, and often earthy, philosophy of their users. They reflect the attitudes and opinions, the truth-in-a-nutshell doctrines, the insights, and condensed wisdom of their time. They also offer us palpable links between past and present: standing as illuminating testimony to the world-view and convictions of our forbears and giving us a heightened, more vital awareness of life today.

1. Proverbs: Universal Truths

During the Middle Ages, and particularly during the Spanish Golden Age, *la sabiduría del pueblo*, or folk-wisdom, was held in high regard and proverbs enjoyed the status of universal truths. The very proverb *los refranes viejos son evangelios pequeños/ breves* (old proverbs are small gospels) itself attests to the way adages were esteemed for the reliability of the doctrines they enshrined. *Don Quijote* is the most shining example of Spanish works of the Golden Age whose prose and verse are richly sprinkled with proverbial dicta, and whose testimony, albeit often swathed in irony, reflects the manner in which adages were employed to prove or disprove the truth of a particular point or argument.

However, in looking at the oral tradition in Spanish proverbs, idioms and slang expressions in this way, we are not endeavouring to investigate whether or not their language chronicles the incontrovertible reality of its time, or envelops historical fact or objective truth. This would be a fruitless task, for such forms of speech teach neither absolute truths nor history. They can, however, give a sense of history: standing as proof of a continuity of thought, of how human nature, with its traits, desires and conduct—the human condition—has changed little down the ages. They reflect the way ordinary people think and speak about the reality of their time. They show that the traditional wisdom and folklore of our ancestors may contain much that is still valid and of worth, such that the popular currency of their maxims still falls from our lips today.

In this book, one of our main purposes is to look at how this colourful, concise and inventive spoken language mirrors the way life is perceived and felt by *el vulgo*, the common man and woman, how it recites their opinions, practical sagacity and beliefs about aspects of their daily life. We also want to contemplate the picture it paints in some of the classics of Spanish literature by looking at examples of the timeless verbal sketches, memorable turns-of-phrase, picaresque wit and folklore depicted therein, and particularly as reflected in some of the most renowned works of the Middle and Golden Ages. For by looking at proverbs and idioms in this way, we can more fully appreciate them in the context of their use, which is, as Erasmus pointed out, a much more satisfactory and profitable way of appreciating the proverb. Erasmus's celebrated collection known as the *Adages*, which first appeared as the *Adagiorum Collectanea* in 1500, endeavoured to demonstrate the dignity and elegance of the proverb as a form of speech. In his commentary on the famous saying *Herculei labores* (in Spanish: *Los trabajos de Hércules*; in English: The labours of Hercules/Herculean task), he speaks of his own labours, and the difficulties he encountered when glossing famous adages. One of the main problems, he explains, resides in the fact that proverbs only show their brilliance when they are being used—not when they are being talked about: «proverbs only show their real beauty when they are inserted like jewels into the right place of speech.»[2]

Separated from this, from their context in speech, when they become mere objects of discussion and research, he says they appear devoid of life, rather petty and flimsy. For this reason, whenever possible we shall be looking at Spanish proverbs and idioms «inserted into the right place»: in the mouths of the people or literary characters whose speech is lit up and enriched by their use.

As mentioned, Cervantes was among many writers of his time who echoed the generally-held belief that every proverb envelops a truth. In Book One of his famous novel, we hear Don Quijote affirm this, using another Spanish adage to prove his point, *no hay refrán que no sea verdadero* (there is no proverb that is not true); this is so, he explains, because they are all rooted in and validated by long experience. Don Quijote uses this proverb when, after suffering great disappointment in one adventure (at the fulling-mills), another opportunity for adventure immediately presents itself. This takes the form of what appears to be a knight, mounted on a dapple-grey horse, riding along wearing Mambrino's fabled gold helmet (but who, in fact, is none other than the local barber, riding an ass, and wearing a brass shaving basin on his head to protect his new hat from the rain). However, as Don Quijote espies a new and daring enterprise in the offing—to challenge the knight and recover the famous helmet—he remarks to his squire Sancho:

> *Paréceme, Sancho, que no hay refrán que no sea verdadero, porque todos son sentencias sacadas de la misma experiencia, madre de las ciencias todas, especialmente aquel que dice: «Donde una puerta se cierra otra se abre.»*[3]

> It seems to me, Sancho, there is no proverb that is not true, because they are all maxims born of experience, mother of all the sciences, especially the one that says: «when one door closes, another opens.»

From the above, we can see how Don Quijote immediately passes from the universal to the particular: illustrating his general point, that there is no proverb that is not true, with a specific example of the way hope usually follows despair, a notion which is encapsulated in the proverb *donde una puerta se cierra otra se abre* (when one door closes, another opens). Thus Quijote demonstrates the veracity and appropriateness of these proverbs in his immediate circumstances.

In fact, this last adage, *donde una puerta se cierra otra se abre*, appears much earlier, a century before Cervantes used it, in Fernando de Rojas' tragi-comedy *La Celestina*, written in 1499. This was a book with which Cervantes was familiar, and which he admired, though he criticized the immoral habits it portrayed, saying it would be "*divi[no] si encubriera más lo huma[no]*" (divine if it veiled some of the more human traits).[4] In *La Celestina* the adage appears in Act XV, in the context of friendly advice given to the troubled servant girl Elicia. Elicia is telling her soul mate, Areúsa, about the deaths of the old procuress, Celestina, and their two young lovers, Sempronio and Pármeno, and Areúsa counsels:

> *Calla, por Dios, hermana, pon silencio a tus quejas, ataja tus lágrimas, limpia tus ojos, torna sobre tu vida. Que cuando una puerta se cierra, otra suele abrir la fortuna, y este mal, aunque duro, se soldará.*[5]

> For God's sake, sister, silence your complaints, cease crying, dry your eyes, look to your life. For when one door closes, fortune usually opens another, and this ill, though hard, will be overcome.

Later, this Spanish proverb found its way into the English language, principally via the influence of the English translations of *Don Quijote* and *Celestina*, but also of *Lazarillo de Tormes*, Spain's first picaresque novel, published in 1554. In this latter, the despair/hope spirit of the adage is alluded to in an inverse sense in the second chapter. Here the starving young *pícaro*, Lazarillo— after thinking he has found some relief to his plight of trying to keep body and soul together—finds that his hopes of obtaining food have been dashed once more by his miserly master, the cleric, and so declares: "... *ciérrase la puerta a mi consuelo y l[a] abriese a mis trabajos.*"[6] (. . . as the door of my consolation closed, [the door] of my troubles opened.)

* * * *

2. Proverbs: Questionable Wisdom

In Spain, as in many other countries, belief in the notion that proverbs were distillations of universal truths, began to be challenged in the 18th century, during the Age of Enlightenment. This was the case particularly among intellectuals and scholastic writers who began to deride the traditional wisdom and folklore that proverbs perpetuated, and dismiss what they considered the frippery of their trite and unrefined, or *vulgar*, language. In England, Swift was a perfect example of this attitude. In 1738, in the Introduction to *Polite Conversation*, he writes "The Reader must learn by all means to distinguish between Proverbs, and those polite Speeches which beautify Conversation . . . As to the former, I utterly reject them out of all ingenious Discourse."[7] In Spain, generally speaking, proverbs and popular speech did not receive such severe criticism, though they were kept at a distance by many intellectuals of the day.

The academic and Cervantes scholar Diego Clemencín writing in the early 1800s, for example, when commenting on the nature of proverbs, praises them for their usefulness as an embellishment of style and admits that some «are of singular merit for the reliability of their maxims, for the shrewdness of their concepts, for the charm of their expression.» But goes on to stress «as to the notion that there is none that is not true, there is much that can be said on this matter . . . Adages are often nothing more than witnesses to the antiquity of errors.»[8] Here Clemencín is probably alluding to the writings on this subject by the erudite eighteenth-century Spanish writer and scholar Fray Benito Jerónimo Feijóo, particularly the latter's essay-letter entitled *Falibilidad de los adagios* (The Falibility of Adages), which, as the title suggests, is a harsh criticism of the credibility of adages.

The Benedictine friar, Feijóo, was an intellectual who had little time for *el vulgo*. He was also scathing in his disapproval of what he saw as the dubious wisdom or truth of many proverbial maxims, which he analysed with an ecclesiastical eye and a syllogistic logic that often bordered on quibbling sophistry. In the first discourse of the first volume of his *Teatro crítico*, he challenges the intuition and common sense attributed to ordinary people, expressed in the maxim: *La voz del pueblo es voz de Dios* (The people's voice is the voice of God). This dictum, he claims, only served to invest the common man with the authority to tyrannize good sense. He maintained that this maxim was the source of numerous other errors, because if one accepts that ordinary people, the multitude, are the measure of truth, then all their errors are thus venerated as inspiration from heaven. Continuing his strictures in *The Falibility of Adages*, he applies his systematic, if convoluted, reasoning, declaring that:

> . . . the proposition that 'the voice of the people is the voice of God', is an adage; therefore I have to accept it as true, because adages are small gospels. What a great argument! Yes, Sir; that the voice of the people is the voice of God is an adage, and that adages are small gospels is another adage, but whoever rejects the truth of the first proposition, perforce must reject the truth of the second. Thus, it is necessary that you, Sir, prove the latter; and if you are only able to prove it by another adage, and even a thousand adages, we are left with nothing; because if for me the attribute of an adage in a proposition does not have the force for it to be accepted as true, the same will be true of any other by that name which you might want me to swallow.[9]

This tortuous reasoning brings to mind the criticism made by the renowned thinker and writer Miguel de Unamuno when he decried some scholastic philosophers' arguments for the existence of God as being full of horrendous thuses and therefores— a system of reasoning that was totally alien to the Gospel itself and to its protagonist. For Christ often used both parables and adages to get his message across: seek and ye shall find; the mote and the beam; man shall not live by bread alone; by their fruits shall ye know them; judge not, that ye be not judged; do unto others. . . ; and so on. As Erasmus once more pointed out, "There are many things in the Gospel that come from the common people."[10] The Sermon on the Mount is brimming with proverbs. Nevertheless, Feijóo keeps up his fault-finding, saying that there are many adages which lack any logical foundation and which are contradictory of one another, a point he goes on to illustrate by citing a list of obscure proverbs that are seemingly either inconsistent, or, according to the scholar, lacking in wisdom. One of the better-known proverbs mentioned in his hit-list is: *Después de comer dormir, después de cenar pasos mil*, an early version of *La comida se reposa, la cena se pasea*, whose English equivalent is: After dinner rest a while, after supper walk a mile, and all of which have their origins in the medieval Latin adage: *Post prandium stabis, post coenam ambulabis*. Regarding this maxim, Feijóo declares that wherever it came from, it is not a piece of advice that is likely to promote good health because:

> . . . movement, when the stomach is full, whether this be after dinner or after supper, is bad. Exercise should be taken not after, but before eating, or at least four or five hours after dinner.[11]

Here Feijóo appears to have overlooked the first piece of advice given in the adage, i.e. that after dinner/lunch (the main and heaviest meal of the day in Spain) one should rest; and after supper (traditionally a lighter meal) one should take a good walk.

He ends his discourse with a warning that there are many more proverbs equally and even more false than the ones he has cited, and all of which appear in Hernán Núñez's famous collection of 1555, entitled *Refranes y proverbios* (Adages and Proverbs). This contained such maxims as:

> *Camino de Roma, ni mula coja, ni bolsa floja*—When going to Rome take neither a lame mule nor an empty purse.

> *Quien es conde y desea ser duque métase fraile en Guadalupe*— If you're a count and want to be a duke, become a friar in the monastery of Guadalupe.

> *Monja para parlar, fraile para negociar, jamás se vio tal par*— A nun for her chatter, a friar for his barter: you'll never see their equal.

> *Al fraile hueco, soga nueva y almendro seco*—For the arrogant/ vain friar, a [hangman's] rope and a dead almond tree.

This last proverb is a curse that refers to the desire to see all conceited friars hanged. Two similar proverb are also recorded later by Correas: *Al fraile, en la horca lo menee el aire* (The friar: let him swing by his neck in the wind); and *El fraile, la horca en el aire* (The friar, the gallows/hangman's rope in the air). Such irreligious adages Feijóo contends are:

... defamatory, scandalous, sacrilegious, because they are slanderous of ecclesiastics (in general), whether members of religious orders or seculars; among which [adages] there are more than a few so erroneous that I still do not know how such injurious dicta against catholic ecclesiastics could have come [even] from the mouth or pen of some heretic.[12]

However, though Feijóo's over-zealous conclusions regarding the trustworthiness of adages may in some cases be true, for most reasonable people the adage's appeal and charm is probably not so much a question of whether or not it enshrines some absolute, irrefutable truth, but more a matter of the utilitarian nature of its wisdom: the sagacity and foresight adages bring to bear in particular cases. A point that was crystallised in Hesiod's epigrammatic remark that 'a popular saying is never meaningless', which is more pertinent, and which, of course, shifts the emphasis somewhat, underlining the contextual appropriateness of the message. As Don Quijote once again said to Sancho on this subject, "*Por cierto, Sancho, ... que siempre traes tus refranes tan a pelo de lo que tratamos ...*"[13] (Well, Sancho, ... you always use proverbs that are most appropriate to our dealings ...). Cervantes may also have been aware of another well-known adage of the time: *los refranes son hermanos bastardos del Evangelio* (proverbs are bastard brothers of the Gospel); *bastardos* perhaps due to the relative or circumstantial truth of their message, overagainst the perceived absolute truth of the Gospel's message.

The contradictory or inconsistent nature of some proverbs when set along side each other emphasizes the point that sayings do not have to encapsulate absolute truths to qualify as proverbs. Two examples of pairs of contradictory Spanish proverbs that immediately spring to mind and which, in one form or another, are common to many languages are:

Más vale quien Dios ayuda que quien mucho madruga—It's better to have God as your helper than to be an early riser.

A quien madruga, Dios le ayuda—lit: God helps the early riser; but equivalent to the English proverb: The early bird catches the worm.

Cuantos más, antes se despacha el trabajo—Many hands make light work.

Muchas manos en un plato hace mucho garabato—Too many cooks spoil the broth.

The paradoxical nature of these proverbs does not necessarily invalidate their message, which is very much dependent on the circumstances or situation to which they refer. In the case of the first pair, both proverbs refer to volition, however in the first one it is the all-powerful Divine Will that is emphasized, and the advantages of those who have God, or luck, on their side; whereas in the second, emphasis is placed on the human will-power needed by the individual in order to reap the rewards that come to an early riser, and who in turn will also receive God's help for his efforts and persistence. It is another version of the adage:

A Dios rogando, pero con el mazo dando—God helps those who help themselves.

In the case of the second pair, the scale of a particular task would bear greatly on the application of the proverbs. When engaged in some detailed and precise work in a confined space like a kitchen, one can see that too many cooks could indeed spoil the dish being prepared; whereas when referring to some large-scale undertaking like, say, painting a house, then, generally speaking, many hands should make the work much lighter.

All of which, brings us back once more to Hesiod's incisive remark that a popular saying is never meaningless, and thus to the utilitarian and relative, or contextual, nature of the wisdom and foresight that proverbial dicta afford.

II

Language and Folklore

1. Proverbs—Linguistic Jewels

Plato, in the *Protagoras*, refers to the value and importance that Socrates placed on the adage as a powerful and sharp rhetorical weapon. In this work Socrates reminds us that Protagoras, considered the wisest and most renowned of the Sophist philosophers (and credited with the dictum 'man is the measure of all things . . . '), very skillfully employed proverbs against his intellectual adversaries to prove his arguments or refute theirs. By this means he was able to disarm them and leave them babbling like children in the face of such rhetorical fire power, for such was the authority of the proverb and the high esteem in which it and its users were held.

Socrates goes on to heap praise on the warrior-like and seemingly brutish Spartans for their skill in the use of adages, and he points to this as a sign of their wisdom, culture and sharpness of mind. Of the same Spartans whom the cultivated Athenians derided for their lack of refinement, Socrates says:

> Now this is how you may know that I am telling the truth and that the Spartans are the best educated in philosophy and speaking: if you talk to the most ordinary Spartan, you will find

that for the most of the time he shows himself a quite unimpressive speaker. But then, ... like a brilliant marksman he shoots in a telling phrase, brief and taut, showing up whoever is talking to him to be as helpless as a child.[14]

The ability to frame such utterances is, Socrates insists, a mark of the highest culture, such that philosophers of the stature of Thales of Miletus, Pittacus, and so on, were "emulators, admirers and disciples of Spartan culture, and their wisdom may be recognized in belonging to the same category, consisting of pithy and memorable dicta uttered by each."[15] Socrates rounds off his praise of the ferocious Spartans, also known as Laconians, by saying "I mention these facts to make the point that, among the ancients, this Laconic brevity was the characteristic expression of philosophy ..."[16]

The technical Spanish term used to refer to the study of proverbs is *paremiología*, from the Greek *paroemia*, meaning adage or by-word. *Paroemia* was also the word Erasmus used, but as Margaret Mann Phillips points out in *The Adages of Erasmus*, this word could "also carry the sense of enigma or parable; when the disciples of Jesus said to their Master 'Lo, now speakest thou plainly, and speakest no proverb' (John XVI, 29) it is the word *paroemia* which is used in the Greek."[17] In this sense, as well as being a pithy saw, *paroemia* could also refer to a dark saying, a truth enswathed in obscurity, that requires interpretation. One of Erasmus's best-known, and most succinct definitions of the adage is: *paroemia est celebre dictum, scita quapiam novitate insigne*, meaning a well-known saying, shrewd and original in conception.

Like Plato, Erasmus also admired the synoptic reasoning and epigrammatic wisdom of the proverb. In the Prolegomena to Section V of the *Adages*, he writes "And in the Proverbs of the ancient world is all its wisdom enshrined."[18] He underscored their wit and succinctness, their allegorical meaning, their often contradictory reasoning, such that we might expect in a riddle. And it is in his commentary on just such a proverbial Latin riddle, *festina lente* (in Spanish: *a gran prisa, gran vagar*; in English: make haste slowly), that he gives perhaps the best definition of the nature and importance of a proverb. Here he writes that in this saying, *festina lente*, we see that:

> The interest of the idea and the wit of the allusion are enhanced
> by such complete neatness and brevity, necessary in my mind to

proverbs, which should be as clear-cut as gems; it adds immensely to their charm. If you consider the force and the significance which are contained in the concision of these words, how fertile, how serious, how wholesome they are and how applicable to every situation in life ...[19]

* * * *

2. Practical and Moral Teaching:

REFRÁN *OR* PROVERBIO

The Spanish language has two words for the English word proverb: *refrán* and *proverbio*. The word *adagio*, or adage, was used in Castile during the Golden Age, as can be seen in the *Tesoro de la lengua castellana* (Treasury of the Spanish Language) by Sebastián de Covarrubias, and of course was the word used by Erasmus from the Latin in his *Adagiorum*. However, although both the words *refrán* and *proverbio* can be used synonymously, and are, in fact, used indistinctly nowadays, the main difference in their meaning is that *refrán* originally referred to a saying or maxim commonly used by ordinary people, while generally speaking, *proverbio* denotes a dictum or adage whose provenance can usually be traced to the classical authors of antiquity. Though these classical dicta were often in oral use long before being recorded on the written page, for many had their origin in some long-forgotten event, person, fable, experience or custom. This distinction in nuance between *refrán* and *proverbio* can be seen clearly in the two medieval works of paroemiology, or treatises on proverbs, by the Spanish compiler and poet, Iñigo López de Mendoza (1398–1458), otherwise known as the Marquis of Santillana. The first of these works with its medieval Spanish title *Refranes que dizen las viejas tras el huego* [sic.] (Sayings Used by Old Women by the Fire) reflects the popular currency of the maxims it records. The second, bearing the flamboyant title *Proverbios de Gloriosa Doctrina e Fructuosa Enseñança* (Proverbs of Golorious Doctrine and Fruitful Teaching), was inspired by and rooted in classical sources and had a clear didactic purpose. It is understandable therefore that the word most used by the Spanish writers whose work was inspired by the realism of every day life was *refrán*, being more *castizo,* or purer, in its traditional currency. The first person to use this word in its primitive form was Arcipreste de Hita at the beginning of the 14TH century. The Archpriest refers to *refranes* as *retraeres* meaning *recuerdos*, or memories, within the Socratic definition that proverbs are laconic, pithy and memorable phrases. The Archpriest too underscores the trustworthiness of *retraeres*—maxims which have been validated by their long and popular oral use and their proven folk wisdom. In his best-known work, *El Libro de Buen Amor* (The Book of Good Love), when introducing a proverb that teaches the uselessness of expending energy on unproductive schemes he writes:

Verdad es lo que dicen los retrares,
quien en el arenal siembra, no trilla pegujares.[20]

It is true what proverbs say,
who sows on sandy ground will reap small return.

As in the above example, such popular sayings are generally introduced in Spanish literary texts as quotations, and/or indicated by any one of such synonyms as: *adagio, aforismo, cantar, decir, dicho, fabla, parlilla, proverbio, refrán, retraer,* as well as other expressions using the verb *decir* (to say), e.g.: *como dice la vieja, como dicen, decir se suele,* etc, (respectively: as the old woman says, as they say, it is often said).

It is difficult to define exactly what constitutes a *refrán* in the Spanish language, as the many works of *paremiología* of the Golden Age and earlier used the term far more loosely than we do nowadays. Such works include similes, popular sayings, descriptive epithets and slang expressions of the time, along side well-known proverbial sentences—the form we expect adages to be couched in today. For example in the *Libro de refranes* (Book of Proverbs), compiled by Mosén Pedro Vallés in 1549—which defines *refranes* as *sentencias breves, sacadas de la lengua y discreta experiencia* (brief maxims drawn from language and judicious experience)— noted proverbs are listed along side colloquial phrases. In this work, the following much-used popular expressions and adages can be found rubbing shoulders with one another:

Eramos trenta, y parió mi abuela—There were already thirty in the family, and grandmother gave birth. The modern-day version of this humorous proverb is the even more droll and ironic: *Eramos pocos, y parió mi abuela* (lit: There were few enough of us, and grandmother gave birth; but meaning: That's all we needed!; As if we didn't have enough problems!) This is used mainly to express the ill-timed increase in the number of people sharing a dwelling which is already overcrowded.

A cada puerco le llega su sanmartín—lit.: St. Martin's day arrives for every pig; meaning: Everyone gets their come-uppance/just deserts in the end. This proverb alludes to the festival of San Martín on 11TH November, a time when it was, and in some areas still remains, the custom in Spain to slaughter pigs in order to prepare pork and ham products for the year.

Cada loco con su tema—Each madman to his own obsession. This proverbial phrase also appears in volume III (205) of the seventeenth-century work *El Criticón* by the witty, *conceptista* writer Baltasar Gracián. In the same volume (183) Gracián uses a different metaphor for this proverb: *Cada lobo por su senda*— Each wolf to his own path. In modern times, the two phrases are conjoined, producing the more memorable rhyme *Cada loco con su tema, y cada lobo por su senda.*

A proverb whose kernel is well-known in many languages, but which in Spanish is particularly graphic is *A dios rogando y con el mazo dando*—lit.: Pleading with God, and still working with the mallet; meaning: God helps those who help themselves.

Another idiomatic expression recorded by Vallés is *pagar el pato*, literally: to pay for the duck, but meaning: to carry the can/ to be left holding the baby. This is typical of the sort of idiom which, when it comes to classifying them, it is difficult to say on which side of the demarcation line between proverbial phrases and slang expressions they lie. The same is also true of such expressions as:

de capa caída—lit.: fallen cape/cloak, but meaning at a low ebb; *caído del cielo*—heaven sent/just the job;

[*no dar*] *pie con bola*—lit.: the foot doesn't make contact with the ball; meaning: can't get anything right;

coger/pegar la hebra—lit.: to pick up the thread; meaning: to go on and on chattering;

como carne y uña—lit.: like flesh and nail; meaning: inseparable/ as thick as thieves. Nowadays this idiom is more commonly heard in the inverse: *como uña y carne*.

However, the Spanish Royal Academy when deciding what exactly constitutes a proverb, applies stricter criteria. Julio Casares, for example, in his *Introducción a la Lexicografía moderna* (Introduction to Modern Lexicography), defines a proverb as:

A complete and independent phrase, that in a direct or allegorical sense, and generally speaking, in a sententious and elliptical form, expresses a thought, a feature of experience, a lesson, a warning, etc., in the form of an opinion in which two ideas are associated.[21]

Yet this definition by the former Secretary of the Spanish Royal Academy, Casares, is clearly far too strict, since it would exclude many proverbs that do not associate or contrast two ideas, but simply employ one allusion. His definition would hold for many Spanish proverbs in binary form, such as:

Dime con quién andas, te diré quién eres—lit.: Tell me with whom you walk, and I'll tell you who you are; but meaning: A man is known by the company he keeps.

Ojos que no ven, corazón que no llora/siente—What the eye doesn't see, the heart doesn't grieve for.

Versions of both the above proverbs are cited in Santillana's fifteenth-century work *Refranes que dicen las viejas*, and Cervantes' *Don Quijote*. However, Casares' over-strict definition would exclude many well-known unidimensional Spanish proverbs such as the following, which are still much used today, and which now form part of *el refranero español* (the body of Spanish proverbs) and appear in most dictionaries of Spanish proverbs:

La codicia rompe el saco—Avarice bursts the sack. A proverb which warns that the greedy who want more, lose everything: Covet all, lose all.

This well-known proverb is found in *Refranes que dicen la viejas* (148), *Quijote* (I, 20; II, 13 and 36), the picaresque novel *Gúzman de Alfarache* (II, 225), and many more famous works of Spanish literature. The same is also true of other well-known adages like:

Poderoso caballero es don dinero—lit.: A powerful lord is Mr Money; meaning: Money is power. A proverb which is closely linked with the name of the seventeenth century writer Francisco de Quevedo, who used it as the refrain in his famous satirical poem of the same title. It still remains one of the most popular proverbs today.

La letra con sangre entra—Instruction enters with blood [sweat and tears]. Found in *Quijote*, and also in the above-mentioned collection of Mosén Pedro Vallés.

Nuestro gozo en el pozo—lit.: Our enjoyment down the well; meaning: That's the end of all our illusions. This idiom appears earlier in *Refranes que dicen las viejas* (499) and in Rojas' *La Celestina* (Act XXI, 293).

* * * *

3. Homespun and Scholarly Wisdom

In the works of the early compilers of proverbs such as the medieval compiler the Marquis of Santillana, and Renaissance paroemiologists like Mosén Pedro Vallés, Hernán Núñez and Juan de Mal Lara, there is a desire to bring together two seemingly opposing strains in both language and wisdom: the popular and the cultured aspects of language, and homespun and scholarly wisdom. Their collections conjoined the erudition, elegance and finely-honed language found in the works of the beloved philosophers and poets of antiquity, and the traditional folk-knowledge, colour and quick idiomatic speech of ordinary people. Each adage chosen was notable for the meaning of its idea, its compressed form and its colourful or distinguished linguistic style.

Referring to the popular element in Santillana's collection *Refranes que dicen las viejas tras el fuego* (Sayings Used by Old Women by the Fire), in the Prologue to the 1910 edition Juan M. Sánchez remarks:

> Just as water is purer the nearer the source from which it springs, so words are more authentic and pure the nearer they are taken from the mouths of ordinary people; this is the case with the *Sayings Used by Old Women*, which the author drank from the fountain of the people, which is always an inexhaustible and rich linguistic mine, a true repository of the most beautiful words that languages treasure and source of turns of phrase, idioms and the nuances of languages.[22]

This drinking at the fountain of the people, to use Sánchez's allusion, and then recording what and how ordinary people think and speak on the written page, either in the great collections of adages, or in the mouths of characters in novels or plays, or indeed in the *coplas* (popular lyric poems and songs) of the time, ensured that so many of these linguistic gems remain on our lips today. We have already had a glimpse of their role as a stylistic device in the works of Cervantes and Rojas, but it should probably be mentioned here that the eternalizing of adages and idioms through the written page has also meant that in many instances it is now almost impossible to distinguish which are of literary origin and which have come directly from the fountain of the people. Many of the proverbs taken from the collections of maxims translated directly from the classics (for example, by the Marquis of Santillana), were often written in verse in the form of *coplas*. And once in song form, the added lyricism usually had the effect of making such maxims more well-known, more popular and all the more memorable for the ordinary person.

One of the most extensive repositories of popular sayings was Gonzalo Correas' *Vocabulario de refranes y frases proverbiales ...* (Collection of Adages and Proverbial Phrases ...), which contains some 18,000 proverbs and idioms, and dates from 1627, though it remained unpublished until the beginning of twentieth century. In the Introduction to the 1924 edition Miguel Mir comments on the copious material and importance of the work, highlighting the way this collection chronicles *lo más castizo*, what is most pure, in the Spanish character, folk-wisdom and language:

> The *Collection* is a treasure-trove of popular wisdom, an archive of what is most pure and brilliant in our language, an immense body of doctrine that lives and beats in the soul of the Spanish people as in no other.

> In effect, in this *Collection*, more than in any other book, is displayed in great profusion the qualities most characteristic of our race: its moral sense, decent or perverted; the liveliness of the imagination, restrained or unbridled; the wit of inventiveness, well or badly directed; all the feelings that have moved our people on all occasions and in all the trials, tribulations and predicaments of their life.[23]

As mentioned earlier, the different sources of Santillana's two collections of adages marks the difference in nuance between the words *refrán* and *proverbio*. In the first work, *Refranes que dicen las viejas* (Saying Used by Old Women), Santillana simply lists the most well-know popular Spanish adages or sayings of *el hogar* (the home), while his collection of *Proverbios de Gloriosa Doctrina* (Proverbs of Glorious Doctrine) was a work designed to have a moral and didactic role, particularly in teaching Christian doctrine to the Prince of Castile, Don Enrique IV, of whose education Santillana was put in charge, by order of the prince's father King Juan II. This work was later glossed by Pedro Díaz de Toledo, who provided erudite commentaries on the classical sources of these adages. The 1787 edition of the work contains a copy of the letter which the Marquis had written to Don Enrique over 300 years earlier, proudly informing the prince that he is not really the "author" of these proverbs, but has taken them from other, more ancient sources, a fact which makes them all the more distinguished and significant:

> . . . if they were to say that I have taken these proverbs, or the greater part of them, from other books, I do not deny it, since I have used the works of Plato, Aristotle, Socrates, Virgil, Ovid, Terence and other philosophers and poets; and I should be most happy for all who read this work to know this, since these very writers took them from others, and they in turn from others,

who arrived at them by experience, a long life and much contemplation.[24]

The 750 sayings contained in *Refranes que dicen las viejas tras el fuego*, (Sayings Used by Old Women by the Fire) formed the basis of all later treatises on proverbs in Spanish, particularly those of the Golden Age. The great significance of Santillana's collection, which recorded the homespun oral wisdom that fell from the lips of old women *en tertulia* (chatting) by the fire, is that a large number of these adages are still in use today. Examples of some of these are:

En boca cerrada no entra mosca (271)—lit: In a closed mouth no fly enters; but meaning: If you keep your mouth shut, you won't put your foot in it. This piece of proverbial sapience has survived until present times in its original form.

A mengua de pan, buenas son tortas (48)—Lacking bread, crackers/cakes will do nicely. The word *torta* nowadays means cake or biscuit, which, in this context (lacking bread), immediately brings to mind Marie Antoinette's remark 'let them eat cake'. However, it is thought that *torta* originally referred to a type of flat, unleavened bread. Another version of this proverb is: *A mengua de carne, buenos son pollos con tocino* (106)— Lacking red meat, chicken and fatty bacon will do nicely. Today the proverb usually runs: *A falta de pan, buenas son tortas*.

A río vuelto, ganancia de pescadores (82)—Much profit may be reaped from confusion. This is an example of an inductive proverb drawn from the particular observation of fishing and widened to situations in everyday life; its literal translation is: a turbulent river is the fisherman's gain. There has been little modification to this proverb down the years, thus the modern-day version is: *A río revuelto, ganancia de pescadores*.

Piensan los enamorados que los otros tienen los ojos quebrados (544)—Lovers think that other people are blind. In the Golden Age, Baltasar Gracián in his emblematic and ideological work *El Criticón* (I, 148) adapted this slightly to: *Piensan los enamorados que todos los demás tienen los ojos vendados*, which has the same meaning and is now the form most often used.

Antes que cases, cata que haces, que no es nudo que así desates (20)—Before you marry, watch what you are doing, for the knot is not easily undone. The English equivalent of this proverb is: Look before you leap. The modern version, recorded by Fernán Caballero in his 19th century work *Lucas García*, discards the second line and runs: *Antes que te cases, mira lo que haces*.

Codicia mala, saco rompe (148)—lit.: Evil avarice bursts the sack; but meaning: Covet all, lose all. This popular proverb with its moral admonition is used in several literary works of the Golden Age, such as: *Guzmán de Alfarache* (II,25) and *Quijote* (II, 13 and 36). In these the maxim appears as it is now best-known: *La codicia rompe el saco*.

Cría el cuervo, sacarte ha el ojo (154)—lit.: Breed a crow and it will pick your eyes out; meaning: To bite the hand that feeds you. This much-used adage, nowadays takes the form: *Cría cuervos y te sacarán los ojos*

Dio Dios habas a quien no tiene quijadas (206)—God gave beans to those who have no jaw. *Habas* (beans) have for centuries been an important part of the Spanish diet, thus it it not surprising that such national habits and customs should be reflected in speech. Beans also feature in another, even more well-known, adage used in *Quijote* (II,13): *En todas partes cuecen habas*—lit.: Beans are cooked everywhere; meaning: It's the same the whole world over.

With regard to the first of these proverbs, over time the reference to beans was changed to almonds, and jawbone replaced by teeth. Thus the adage now runs: *Da Dios almendras al que no tiene muelas*—God gives almonds to those who have no teeth. It is curious that a proverb with such a long heritage seems not to have appeared in the English language until the early nineteenth century. In English it runs: God sends nuts to those who have no teeth. A more colourful variant in Spanish is the one often heard in Andalucía: *Da dios mocos al que no tiene pañuelo*—God gives a snotty nose to those who have no handkerchief.

Cada uno dice de la feria como le va en ella (155)—lit.: Each person speaks of the fair according to how it went for him;

meaning: Speak as you find. This proverbs reflects the importance of the fair in an agricultural society. Fairs originally had
both a social and a commercial purpose—a market and meeting
place for people from the surrounding areas, where they could
buy and sell animals and food and other goods, as well as
exchange news and gossip. It is only in more recent times that
fairs came to mean a local *fiesta* where people could dance or
enjoy fairground games and rides, etc. In Act IV of the famous
tragi-comedy *La Celestina*, written in 1499, the young heroine
Melibea uses the proverb when speaking to the procuress
Celestina, saying: "*Bien conozco que hablas de la feria según
te va en ella: así que otra canción dirán los ricos.*" (I can well
see that you speak of the fair according to how it went for you:
so I suppose the rich will sing a different song.) The modern
version is: *Cada uno habla/cuenta de la feria como le va
en ella.*

Obras son querencias (505)—Deeds are love. In *El Criticón* this
appears as *Obras son amores*, and it is one of the few cases of
a laconic adage having lengthened with time, since it now runs:
Obras son amores, que no buenas razones—Love is works
not words.

Dime con quién andabas y decirte he qué hablabas (200)—lit:
Tell me with whom you were walking, and I'll tell you about
what you were talking; meaning: A man is known by the company he keeps. In *Quijote* (II, 10 and 23) the proverb is trans-
posed into the present tense and the verb to speak (*hablar*) is
changed to *ser* meaning 'to be' which denotes identity, thus:
Dime con quién andas, decirte he quién eres—Tell me with
whom you walk, and I'll tell you who you are, which is almost
identical to the modern day version: *Dime con quién andas, te
diré quién eres.*

Más vale pájaro en mano que buitre volando (422)—lit.:
Better a bird in the hand than a vulture in flight; meaning: A
bird in the hand is worth two in the bush. Another version,
perhaps even more well known is: *Más vale pájaro en mano
que ciento volando*—A bird in the hand is worth a hundred in
flight. An even more surreal variant found in the picaresque
novel *Guzmán de Alfarache* (III, 259) substitutes ox (*buey*) for

vulture, thus: *Más vale pájaro en mano que buey volando*—Better a bird in the hand than an ox in flight.

Bien canta Marta cuando está harta (114)—Martha sings well on a full stomach. This proverb, advocating that it is easier to work when well nourished, has remained unchanged and is still used in this form today. It is reminiscent of the English saying: An army marches on its stomach.

Muera gata y muera harta (417)—Let the cat die with its belly full. A slightly different version is used in *Quijote* (II, 59). In this scene Don Quijote, after being trampled by a herd of bulls and bullocks, finds he has lost his appetite. However, he tells the ever-hungry Sancho to go and eat for he is aware that though he himself was born to live dying, Sancho was born to die eating. To this his squire remarks that in that case "*no aprobará vuesa merced aquel refrán que dice «muera Marta, y muera harta»*" (your worship will therefore not approve of the proverb that says: Let Marta die, but die with her belly full).

Quien bien quiere a Baltrán, bien quiere a su can (613)—lit: Who well loves Beltran, well loves his dog; meaning: Love me love my dog. When the proverb appears in *Celestina* (Act XVII, 267) it loses the metaphor of the dog and the second part of the maxim is expanded to cover everything that Beltran possesses: *Quien bien quiere a Beltrán, a todas sus cosas ama*—Who dearly loves Beltran, loves all his things.

For a more extensive selection of the proverbs compiled by the Marquis of Santillana in *Refranes que dicen las viejas tras el fuego*, see the last section of the book.

PROVERBS OF GLORIOUS DOCTRINE . . .

Santillana's other collection *Proverbios de Gloriosa Doctrina y Fructuosa Enseñanza* (Proverbs of Glorious Doctrine and Fruitful Teaching), looked to classical writers of antiquity for its didactic inspiration, writers such as: Solomon, Socrates, Plato, Seneca, Tulio, Varerio, Aristotle and Cato. These Santillana glossed in verse in the form of *coplas de pie quebrado* (poems or songs of octosyllabic lines interspersed with a half line). As mentioned, the work was commissioned specially by King Don Juan II for the education of his son, the Prince of Castile, Don Enrique IV. However, though these adages were taken mainly from pre-Christian sources, they were glossed with the ideology of Christian moral spirituality. Thus the so-called Platonic or Aristotelian thoughts expressed in such adages cannot be understood in their original context or sense, but via Santillana's medieval Christian interpretation of these. The result is an amalgamation of pre-Christian systematic thought and the moral doctrines of the early Fathers of the Church. The cultured language of the *Proverbios* contrasts sharply with the more down-to-earth speech of his *Refranes*. For this reason, the *Proverbios* did not strike such a familiar chord in the imagination of ordinary people and thus have had far less resonance in the Spanish language. Nevertheless, they played an important didactic role in underscoring the tenets of Christian morality, particularly as they were dressed in memorable rhyming verse. Some examples of these in their original medieval Spanish are given below:

1

Fijo mío mucho amado,	Dearest son of mine,
Para mientes,	Stop and think,
Que non contrastes	Do not judge people
* las gentes*	
Mal su agrado:	Badly for their liking:
Ama y serás amado,	Love and you will be loved,
E farás	And you will do
Lo que facer no podrás	All that you could not do
Desamado.	Unloved.

4

Quntos vi ser aumentados	How many have I seen elevated
Por amor;	By love;
E muchos mas por themor	And how many more by fear
Abaxados! ...	Diminished! ...
Ca los buenos, sojugados	For the good, subjugated,
Non tardaron	Do not take long
De buscar como libraron	To find a way to free themselves
Sus estados.	From their state.

15

A los libres perteneçe	To the free belongs
El aprender	Learning,
Dónde se muestra el saber	Where knowledge is reflected
E floreçe;	And flourishes;
Çirtamente bien mereçe	Certainly well worthy of
Preheminençia	Preeminence
Quien de doctrina e prudençia	Is he who with doctrine and prudence
Se guarneçe.	Adorns himself.

18

Si fueres grant eloquente	If you be grandiloquent
Bien será;	So be it;
Pero no te converná	But it does not suit you
Ser prudente:	To be prudent:
Que el prudente es obediente	For the prudent man is obedient
Toda via	In every way
A moral filosofía	To moral philosophy
E sirviente.	And is its servant.

35

Quanto es bueno el comer	How good it is to eat
Por medida,	In moderation,
Que sostiene nuestra vida	For it keeps our life
De caer,	From fading,
Tanto es de aborreçer	How detestable is
El gloton,	The glutton,
Que piensa er perfection	Who thinks that perfection is
El tal plazer.	Found it that pleasure.

38

Tiempo se deve oto [r] gar	Time should be given
Al aprender,	To learning,
Que no se adquiere saber	For knowledge is not acquired
Sin trabajar.	Without work.
Assi deves hordenar	So should you order
El tu vivir,	Your way of life,
Que pospongas mal dormir	Pay no heed to sleeping badly
Por bien velar.	So as to keep a good vigil.

The inter-relationship between the proverb and the popular and cultured strains in literature and language was from the outset an important focus of attention for Spanish paroemiologists. Santillana was the first to compile and gloss the wisdom enshrined in classical adages and popular sayings. But it was, above all, the influence of Erasmus's *Adages* that sparked the major treatises on proverbs in Spain. However, Erasmus was to focus on the humanistic and didactic value of adages taken mainly from classical sources, whereas the works of the early Spanish compilers also pay homage to the humanistic values reflected in the synoptic reasoning and plain-spoken sapience of ordinary people. An aspect that was crystallized in the works of the most renowned writers of the Golden Age, for whom proverbial dicta became an indispensable literary device, as we shall see in more detail later in Section V.

III

Oral Tradition in Idioms, Proverbs and Slang

1. Types of Proverbs

Proverbs can fall into one or more of several categories. The principal categories are listed below, together with examples of proverbs that fall into each. The proverbs themselves are followed by a brief parenthetical note mentioning the name of some of the most renowned authors and works to have used them.

DEDUCTIVE PROVERBS

These comprise abstract statements which express some general truth about life, for example:

Vanse los amores y quedan los dolores—Lovers leave and pain remains. This proverb cautions that passionate love is a thing of short duration and once the flame dies, the pain of love remains long after. The poet Gil Vicente (c.1470–c.1536) alludes to this adage in his *cantiga de amor* (medieval lyric poem set to music) *Vanse mis amores*, the first stanza of which is:

Vanse mis amores	My love has gone
Vanse mis amores, madre,	Mother dear, my love has gone

luengas tierras van morar.	To distant lands there to dwell.
Yo no los puedo olvidar.	I can't forget, hear my plea:
¿Quién me los hará tornar?	Who will bring him back to me?
¿Quién me los hará tornar?	Who will bring him back to me?

En las dolencias de amor, olvidar es lo mejor—lit.: In the pains of love, it's better to forget. This Spanish saying originally appeared in the *canción* (lyric poem) by Cristóbal de Castillejo (c.1490–1550). This is written in traditional octosyllabic lines, in full rhyme:

Olvidar es lo mejor	'Tis better to forget
En las dolencias del amor,	With love's most woeful debt,
de pesar o de placer,	Whether pain or pleasure,
al que lo puede hacer,	When weighed by good measure,
olvidar es lo mejor.	'Tis better to forget.

Es amor una locura	Love is a madness, to be sure,
de tristeza o de alegría,	Whether it be sadness or joy,
que con memoria se cría	And nurtured by memory's ploy,
y con olvidar se cura;	Only forgetting can inure.
el hurgarle es lo peor,	To scratch it with danger's beset,
porque para guarecer	For while clinging to life's treasure,
al que lo puede hacer,	When weighed by good measure,
olvidar es lo mejor.	'Tis better to forget.

Del decir al hacer mucho hay—Between saying and doing there's an abyss. This was recorded as early as the end of the thirteenth century in the first Spanish romance of chivalry entitled *El libro del Caballero Zifar* (The Book of the Knight Zifar, 198). Another adage with a similar message, and which is much used nowadays, is: *del dicho al hecho hay mucho trecho*—it's easier said than done. [*Quijote*, II, 34 and 64].

El bien no es conocido hasta que es perdido—You don't know a good thing until you've lost it. [Santillana, *Refranes que dicen las viejas*, 487; Mateo Alemán, *Guzmán de Alfarache*, I, 168].

Inductive proverbs often convey homespun wisdom, drawn from particular observations of everyday life, and teach or make a general point. The subject-matter and imagery used in many of these adages often means that they stride both this and the category of proverbs that relate to rural knowledge, i.e. folk wisdom that was built up in a pre-industrial society. The following are much-used examples of this type:

Por el hilo se saca el ovillo—lit: The ball of yarn is unwound by the thread; meaning: It's a question of putting two and two together. [*Quijote*, I, 4 and 30; II, 12].

De noche todos los gatos son pardos—At night all cats are grey. This proverb cautions that in the dark it is easier to hide any faults a thing might have. [*Quijote*, II, 3 and 23].

A río revuelto, ganancia de pescadores—lit: A turbulent river is the fisherman's gain; a proverb teaching that much profit may be reaped from confusion. [*Celestina*, Act II, 99. Also recorded in *Refranes que dicen las viejas*, Santillana; and in *Libro de refranes* by Mosén Pedro Vallés.]

Quien con perros se echa, con pulgas se levanta—Who sleeps with dogs, awakes with fleas. [*Zifar*, 336]. This warns that imprudent actions can only produce adverse results. Another, more modern version of this proverb is: *Quien con niños se acuesta, cagado amanece*—Who sleeps with the baby, awakes shitty.

CLASSICAL PROVERBS EXPRESSED IN THE VERNACULAR

These often encapsulate kernels of traditional knowledge, folklore or legend from particular countries or regions:

Cada gallo canta en su muladar—Every cock will crow upon his own dunghill. The Stoic philosopher Seneca (born in the Andalusian city of Cordoba during the early Roman Empire) was the first to record this proverb in Latin as: *Gallum in suo sterquilinio plurimum posse* (the cock is most powerful upon his own dunghill), in *Apocolocyntosis*, vii. [This was first recorded in Spain in *Refranes que dicen las viejas*, 159; also included in *Refranes y máximas populares...*, 263, by the nineteenth-century writer Fernán Caballero.]

Del mal, el menos—Of two evils choose the less. First found in Aristotle's *Ethics* II,ix. 1109a; and Cicero in *De Officiis*, III, xxix, as *minima de malis*. [In Spain:Arcipreste de Hita, *Libro de Buen Amor*, v.1617; *Guzmán de Alfarache*, much cited, e.g. II, 101.]

Más vale tarde que nunca—Better late than never. Used by Dionysius of Halicarnassus in *Roman Antiquities*, ix,9.

Ayúdate bien, y ayudarte ha Dios—God helps them that help themselves. First found in Aeschylus, *Fragments*, 395. [In Spain: *Zifar*, 199; *Refranes y máximas populares...*, 264.] Another version of this proverb in Spanish is: *Quien se guarda, Dios le guarda*—God looks after those who look after themselves. [*Zifar*, 398.]

MORAL PROVERBS

These often advise on correct action and caution against wrong behaviour. A vast number of proverbs fall under this heading, many of Biblical origin. The Gospel of St. Matthew is a particularly rich source, especially in the Sermon on the Mount. Most of the maxims in this group are relatively straightforward and require little or no explanation, since they have a similar format in many languages.

Quien busca, halla—Seek and ye shall find.

La fe sin obras muerta es—Faith without works is dead. [Arcipreste de Talavera (1398–c.1470), *Corbacho*, 96.] However this was first recorded by St Paul in *Epistolae Iacobi*, 2,17. as: *Sic et fides, si non habeat opera, mortua est in semetipsa.*

La codicia rompe el saco—Avarice bursts the sack. This teaches that the greedy who have much and want more end up losing all. [*Guzmán de Alfarache*, II, 225; *Quijote*, I, 20; II, 13 and 36].

A Dios rogando, y con el mazo dando—lit.: Pleading with God, but still working with the mallet, meaning: God helps them that help themselves. [*Quijote*, II, 35 and 71]. This is another version of *ayúdate bien, y ayudarte ha Dios*, as seen above.

Aquel es rico, que está bien con Dios—He is rich who is in God's favour. [*Celestina* Act IV, 116].

Hacer bien, nunca se pierde—A good need is never lost. [Lope de Vega, *La Dorotea*, 230]

METAPHORICAL PHRASES EXPRESSED AS PROVERBS

The Spanish language displays an abundance of this type of colourful adage. Among the most well-known are:

Aunque la mona se vista de seda, mona se queda—An ape's an ape, a varlet's a varlet, though they be clad in silk and scarlet; another version of: you can't make a silk purse out of a sow's ear. A famous proverb of classical provenance, first found in Lucian's *Adversus Indoctum* 4. [In Spain: *Guzmán de Alfarache*, II, 115]

En boca cerrada no entra mosca—lit.: In a closed mouth no fly enters; meaning: If you keep your mouth shut, you won't put your foot in it. [*Refranes que dicen las viejas*, 271]. Correas, in his *Vocabulario de refranes* lengthens the proverb slightly, making it even more graphic: *En boca cerrada no entra ni mosca ni araña*—lit: in a closed mouth neither fly nor spider enters.

En tierra de ciegos, el tuerto es rey—In the land of the blind, the one-eyed man is king. [*Criticón*, II, 370] This proverb appears in Erasmus's *Adages* in its Latin form: *in regione caecorum rex est luscus*.

Dijo la sartén a la caldera: quítate allá, culinegra—lit.: As the frying pan said to the kettle: move out of the way, black-bottom. [*Refranes que dicen las viejas*, 215; *Quijote*, II, 67.] An English version of this proverbial phrase is: the pot calling the kettle black.

These originated in a largely agricultural society, and allude to such things as customs, food, nature, the seasons, weather, husbandry, etc:

Cantarillo que muchas veces va a la fuente, o deja el asa o la frente—lit.: The pitcher that goes to the spring often either leaves the handle or the lip behind; meaning: You should not push your luck too far. [*Zifar*, 416; *Refranes que dicen las viejas*, 143; *Quijote*, I, 30; *Refranes y máximas populares*, 256] A more modern version of this popular proverb is: *Tanto va el cantaro a la fuente que al fin se rompe*—The pitcher goes to the spring so often that it ends up broken.

A cada puerco le llega su sanmartín—lit.: St. Martin's day arrives for every pig; meaning: Everyone gets their comeuppance/just deserts in the end. As mentioned earlier, this proverb alludes to the the period, around the festival of San Martín on 11th November, when it was, and in many places still remains, the custom to carry out *la matanza* (the slaughter of pigs) in order to prepare fresh meat, *embutidos*, or sausages, cured hams and salt-pork, along with the products made from the offal. [*Refranes que dicen las viejas*, 532. Also recorded in *Libro de refranes* by Vallés.]

Huyendo del perejil, le nació en la frente—lit.: Running from the parsley, it grew on his forehead; meaning: Out of the frying pan into the fire. [*Refranes que dicen las viejas*, 350; *Guzmán de Alfarache*, V, 62.]. A modern variant of this much-used adage, and one that still uses rural imagery is: *Huyendo del perejil, dio en el berenjenal*—lit.: Running from the parsley, he landed in the aubergine bed.

En casa del herrero, cuchillo de palo—lit.: In the blacksmith's house, a wooden knife; meaning: The family of a skilled person are often the last to enjoy the benefits of his trade. [*Refranes que dicen las viejas*, 281]. Versions of this proverb in English are: the shoemaker's son/wife always goes barefoot; and there's none worse shod than the shoemaker's wife.

Buñolero solía ser; volvíme a mi menester—lit.: A baker I used to be; I went back to my trade; meaning: every man to his trade. [*Refranes que dicen las viejas*, 694; *Guzmán de Alfarache*, II, 99].

ENIGMATIC OR PROBLEMATIC PROVERBS

These employ seemingly contradictory reasoning, and are often couched in the form of a riddle or enigmatic phrase, for instance:

Aquel sabe del bien, que sabe del mal—lit.: He knows the good, who knows the bad; meaning: A person who has experienced bad times, is better able to value the good times. [*Criticón*, III, 290.] A more overt form of this adage is: *Quien no sabe de mal, no sabe de bien*—He who has not experienced bad times, cannot appreciate good times. [*Refranes y máximas populares*, 257.]

A gran prisa, gran vagar—Make haste slowly. Another form of this proverb which is much used today is: *Si tienes prisa, vístete despacio*—If you're in a hurry, dress slowly. As mentioned earlier, this is a version of the classical Latin adage *festina lente*, a proverb that Erasmus called truly royal. This was so, he claimed, firstly because of the wisdom of its message and secondly, because it is precisely the minds of princes that are most prone to flout its teaching. Once the camouflage of the riddle's husk (the seeming contrariness) has been removed, the kernel of its teaching, according to the Dutch scholar, is: ". . . a wise promptness together with moderation, tempered with vigilance and gentleness, so that nothing is done rashly and then regretted, and nothing useful to the common weal omitted out of carelessness . . ."[25]

El que come más, come menos—He who eats a lot, eats less. This proverb teaches that the person who eats to excess will have a short life. It also alludes to the notion that the person who wastes his fortune ends by living in straitened circumstances. [*Criticón*, I, 217.]

A la vejez, viruelas—In old age, chickenpox. The laconic brevity and wit of this well-known adage take a swipe at those who, in advanced years, behave (particularly in the sphere of love), or dress in an inappropriate manner. In the fifteenth century, Santillana recorded another proverb with a similar meaning that mocked elderly men who dyed their hair so as to appear younger: *A la vejez, aladares de pez*—lit.: In old age, gills of a fish. The word *aladares* refers to the hair on both sides of the head that is combed forward over the temples, but figuratively it refers to a fish's gills.

El mucho bien hace mal—Too much good is bad. This adage counsels that too much good living, or too much kindness often has bad results. [*Criticón*, I, 218.]

Si quieres vivir mucho y sano, hazte viejo temprano—If you want to live a long and healthy life, become old early. This proverbial riddle advises that the best way to ensure a long and healthy life is to adapt the prudent life style and epicurean habits of the elderly.

2. The Cut and Thrust of a Sharp Tongue

La lengua callejera, or slang, in many cultures has long been a means by which the masses, the down-trodden and the marginalized could subvert the established order by subjecting it to derision in a *vulgar tongue*—which, more often than not, is also a sharp tongue, whose inventiveness and wit therefore cuts and wounds its target more deeply. The derision dished out in irreverent criticism, mockery, satirical humour, and sarcastic tags is the sort of abuse that immediately ups the ante, adding more spice, colour, weight and imagery to the language of protest, thereby making it that much more memorable and hence effective. Slang is the cutting-edge of language where creativity and versatility twist meanings to attack hypocrisy. It plays on words to sabotage sham sanctimoniousness, paints irreverent pictures to deflate overblown pomposity, and mocks the cant and pretentiousness of the prevailing morals. It tells the establishment that *bien sabemos de qué pie cojeas* (we know which foot you limp on: we know where you're coming from/ we know your faults and weaknesses). It shows us, *el vulgo*, the common man and woman, that we are not alone in our thoughts or ideas, or in our disdain for our rulers or *betters* and the institutions they represent—whether of Church or State—for often *cojean del mismo pie* (they limp on the same foot: have the same faults). And of the rest, *el que no cojea, renquea* (he who doesn't limp, hobbles: no one is perfect). Thus if they, the establishment, can be mean in their ways and edicts, then we can at least be mean with our tongues to expose the humbug they embody. For, as the proverb goes, *cada renacuajo tiene su cuajo* (even the smallest frog can croak). In the people's unrefined mouths the tongue may be a vulgar sword, but this only sharpens its cutting edge and increases its penetration. (Many examples of much-used Spanish slang terms and expressions can be found in Sections IV and VII.)

3. Censorship and the *Vulgar* Tongue

It is perhaps at those times when a particularly oppressive, authoritarian rule is exercised over a country and its people, and where censorship is the order of the day, that the oral tradition takes on greater significance, mainly because the spoken word is much more difficult to control than the written word. In the case of Spain, two examples of such times immediately come to mind. One being the dictatorial regime of General Franco (1939–1975); the other, the period in which Inquisitorial control was at its severest when censorship was tightened by the establishment of the *Index Librorum Prohibitorum* (the Index of Prohibited Books) in 1559. This latter remained in force until its abolition in 1813 by The Cortes of Cadiz (The Spanish Parliament which sat in Cadiz from 1810–1813). Such periods gave added impetus to the inventive *lengua picaresca*, or picaresque language and wit of the Spanish people. Imaginative linguistic ciphers and dissembling verbal communication offered a means of criticizing, protesting against and denouncing the established order—a means which, as mentioned, is much more difficult to constrain than the written word.

Such rhetorical weapons as the satirical verses and *coplas* of the carnival songs, scoffing adages, proverbial warnings and irreverent jokes, may not have been sticks and stones, but they were words that certainly hurt and got their message across. In fact there is an old saying which itself attests to the success of the *copla* as an excellent means of communication: *andar en coplas*, meaning something that is made the subject of a popular song and thus is made common knowledge. It is equivalent to the modern-day idiom *salir en los periódicos* (to have one's name/picture plastered over the newspapers/be given a bad press). This is the glory, and often the gory, of the oral tradition, of the inventive and ever-evolving spoken language—but much of which, we have to admit, would not have survived without the written word.

IV

A Spanish Philosophy of Life— The People's Voice

In this section we shall examine the way Spanish folklore—the way of being and seeing the world—is reflected in language, and in particular in popular speech. We shall look briefly at the philosophical roots that have had a special influence on Spanish thought and life, and hence on language; and examine the role paradox and contradiction play in understanding the Spanish conception of life and way of speaking about it. This is illustrated by an analysis of the use of religious symbolism in colloquial speech, and, in particular, in the mixture of religious and profane expressions which produce a language rich in colour, crude metaphor and picaresque wit. This focus, we trust, will help illuminate the Spanish vision of the world and give a better understanding of the nation's folklore and philosophy of life.

1. Spanish Popular Speech—A Mirror of its People

One of the first questions that arises when approaching this subject, is whether in fact we can speak of a conception of life that is markedly Spanish? Can we identify a Spanish philosophy, or way of thinking, that manifests itself in the nation's folklore? Folklore understood in its original sense: folk, meaning people, nation, race, or nowadays "the ordinary people"; and lore, meaning the traditional beliefs and conception of life that underpin a distinct view of the world. And if so, how is this philosophy and folklore reflected in language and, in particular, in popular speech?

As the guiding principle here we have followed the advice given by the nineteenth-century Spanish folklorist Antonio Machado Alvarez (father of the famous poet) when he said:

> Study ordinary people, who without grammar or rhetoric, speak better than you, because they express the whole of their thought without adulterations or sleight of hand; and they sing better than you, because they say what they feel. The people, not academies, are the true conservers of the language and the real poets of the nation.[26]

Following Machado's counsel, we shall focus our attention on the direct observation of what *el vulgo* says: the use of colloquial speech—slang, idioms and proverbs employed, and the context in which they are used.

Language in general, and popular speech in particular, is not only a way of communicating, but also an expression of the collective spirit of a people, nation, or region. It is a true reflection of the way they interpret life, their scale of values, way of being and folklore: their philosophy of life. For when we philosophize, we think in words, in language, "our" language. As the well-known writer and thinker Miguel de Unamuno cannily asked: "But is it possible to philosophize in pure algebra, or even in Esperanto?" Of course not, "history is not mathematics, nor is philosophy." Language, as Unamuno went on to explain, is a social and racial product, "*y raza, la sangre del espíritu, es lenguaje.*" (and race, the blood of the spirit, is language.)[27]

As we have seen, an old Spanish proverb runs: *Dime con quién andas y te diré quién eres*, (literally: tell me with whom you walk and I'll tell you who you are; but which is equivalent to the English proverb: A man is known by the company he keeps). In the context of this study, we should like to change this proverb to the following: *Dime qué hablas y te diré quién eres* (Tell me what you say, and I'll tell you who you are). For what we say is the mirror that reflects the essence of our personality and our conception of life.

And this brings us back once more to our first catena of questions: can we speak of a conception of life that is markedly Spanish? Can we identify a way of philosophizing and a folklore that reveal a distinct Spanish view of the world?

In order to answer these questions, and before entering into a direct analysis of the language of popular speech, we first of all want to sketch out what we see as the background, or philosophical roots and influences that have been the seed bed and fertilizer of the present-day linguistic fruits which are the subject of our attention.

Unamuno, in his essay entitled *Ganivet Filósofo* (Ganivet, Philosopher), published in 1903, contends:

> Our [Spanish] philosophy, if one can call it that, cannot be squeezed into logical pigeon-holes: it must be sought incarnate in fictional deeds and in carved images, in *Life is a Dream* or in *Don Quijote*.[28]

This philosophy Unamuno calls *una filosofía líquida*, a "liquescent" philosophy, that is to say, one that is diffused throughout the nation's literature, life, mysticism and language; a way of thinking, that cannot be pinned down and labeled, or squeezed into logical pigeon-holes.[29] Furthermore, it is a philosophy whose genealogy can be traced to the early seeds scattered by Stoicism and which embedded themselves deep in Spanish soil and consciousness.

The Stoic influence, especially that of the later Stoics such as Epictetus and Seneca, has had a special resonance on Spanish life. (Seneca was, in fact, born in the Andalusian city of Cordoba during the early Roman Empire, when the city belonged to the Roman province known as Betica.) The influence of these thinkers on Spanish thought, and thus language, is evidenced throughout Spanish literature and especially so in the works of the 17th century writer Calderón de la Barca. For the Spanish mind, (as for Seneca, who believed philosophy was the science of conduct) philosophy is essentially about people and the practical, not abstract logic and theoretical investigation. And people cannot be dealt with, pigeon-holed, by systems. As heard recently, when travelling by bus from Seville to Jerez, in an exchange between two young men:

— *"Anda, que te tienen fichado."*
— *"¿A mí fichado? A mí no me ficha ni Dios."*

— "Come off it! They've got you sussed."
— "Me sussed?—I'm not even in God's filing cabinet."

This exchange is also a perfect example of the nature of popular speech: it employs words and symbols that are specific to a particular people, and the play on words, colour and humour are often lost in translation. As here above, *fichado* is a play on words between being sussed/found out and being filed. And this difference in verbal and cultural reference is a problem we shall encounter when trying to translate other idiomatic expressions as we go along.

Stoic concepts have had a great influence on the Spanish way of being and seeing the world and have been an inspiration for much of the country's literature, particularly Epictetan concepts, whereby the individual person, *persona* or *prosopon* (the Greek term used by Epictetus to signify the mask worn by an actor on stage) is viewed as an actor who plays out a given role in life's drama. As the playwright Calderón de la Barca so graphically expresses: "come, mortals, come and bedeck yourselves one and all to perform on the stage of the world".[30] This age-old metaphor of life viewed as a brief theatrical appearance, acted out on a grand world stage—the question of reality versus illusion—has been a constant theme of philosophy and literature throughout the ages. Added to this notion of the human individual as a player who performs a predestined role on life's stage, is another all-important Epictetan doctrine: that of the primacy of the will. This is a concept which plays a central role throughout Spanish philosophy and folklore, precisely because of its bearing on such major existential themes as anthropocentricity, autonomy, authenticity, freedom, decision, etc., a doctrine that rests on the idea that the individual will is completely autonomous. Furthermore, it is a doctrine that has been much neglected when reference is made to Stoic thought, for emphasis is almost invariably placed on the deterministic element: acceptance of what life and the laws of nature (destiny) decree.

With reference to the deterministic element, there are many examples of this in well-known proverbs and modern-day idioms, which for the most part tend to be of an earthy nature. The following are just a few examples of this:

Unos nacen con una estrella y otros estrellados—lit: Some are born under a [lucky] star, others seeing stars; meaning: Fate/Fortune smiles on some but not on others.

El hombre propone, y Dios dispone—Man proposes, and God disposes/decides.

Matrimonio/Cuna y mortaja, del cielo bajan—lit: Marriage/Cradle and shroud, from heaven come down; meaning: All things of this world are ordained by fate/heaven.

Mi marido es tamborilero; Dios me lo dio y así me lo quiero—My husband is a drummer; God gave him to me and I love him as he is. [as God gave him to me]

El mal que no tiene cura, ni el cura—lit: The illness that has no cure, not even the priest; meaning: There are no cures for ill fate.

Cuando mucho llueve, ¿qué hemos de hacer sino dejarla caer?—When it pours with rain, what can we do but let it fall?

Cada uno estornuda como Dios le ayuda—Each person's sneeze is as God decrees.

Acá y allá, Dios dirá—Down here or up there, God ordains.

A quien Dios quiere bien, la perra le pare lechones.—Whom God loves well, his dog will have a litter of piglets. Again, this indicates that a person's good luck depends on God's will.

One of the most frequently heard deterministic idioms is:

Me tocó la china, ¡qué le vamos a hacer!—I drew the short straw/had bad luck, but there's nothing I can do about it.

And in its colourful Andalusian version:

Como te caiga un mal fario, vas de culo.—meaning something like: If you're struck by bad luck, you go arse first [you can't do anything about it]. *Fario* is an Andalusian word whose expressiveness both in meaning and in the way it is enunciated is charged with foreboding—it seems to fill the whole mouth with air ready to be spat out like a bad spell.

Another Andalusian expression with a similar sentiment is:

Volvérsele el santo de espaldas—lit: The saint turns his back on her/him; meaning: Someone's luck has changed for the worse.

The above are a few sayings or idioms reflecting the deterministic element. But the equally important, though clearly totally contradictory element in Stoic philosophy, i.e. that of the autonomous will, is for some reason often forgotten when discussing Stoic thought, perhaps because it is so obviously incompatible with the first, deterministic, element. For the philosopher Epictetus, the individual will lies entirely within the human being's own power. Thus neither predestination nor any outside power can force the individual to do anything against his own will. As Epictetus remarked: "What say you, fellow? Chain me? My leg you will chain—yes, but not my will—no, not even Zeus can conquer that."[31]

Or, as I heard an elegantly-dressed woman, watching the processions of Holy Week in the Andalusian city of Cadiz, remark:

"*Pues, díselo a quien te dé la gana que, aunque me lo pida el "greñuo", no lo hago.*"
"Well you can tell whom the hell you like, but even if the *greñuo* himself asks me, I refuse to do it."

Fortunately, I knew what *greñuo* referred to, though not many people outside the Cadiz region would. *Greñuo* (*greñudo*) means someone with long, tangled hair. But here it refers to the nickname for Christ the Nazarene, a rather hippy-looking statue of Christ, wearing a wig of long, dishevelled hair. The statue is carried in procession along the streets in the middle of the night on Maundy Thursday. Thus, like Epictetus, our elegant lady in Cadiz was saying that not even God, Christ himself (*el greñuo*) could force her to do something against her will. Perhaps two of the most potent expressions indicating radical voluntarism are the Andalusian sayings:

¡*El Cristo al río!*—lit: Into the river with Christ!; but meaning: Nobody/Not even Christ can stop me!

Echar los cristos a rodar—To set/let off Christs; meaning: To display a violent temper [in order to get one's way].

It is also very common to make comparisons with God or Christ in Spanish, either equating a person with God or making the individual's will stronger than God's. For example, when equating someone with God you can hear:

Estuviste como Dios.—You were like God. This refers to an outstanding performance in some sphere of life.

Armaste la de Dios or *Armaste la de Dios es Cristo*—lit: To cause that of God/that of God is Christ; but meaning: You raised hell/caused a tremendous fuss.

Ni Cristo pasó de la cruz, ni yo paso de aquí—Christ didn't move from the cross, and I'm not moving from here. [Indicating wilful intransigence].

Making someone's will superior to God's is often encountered in common expressions such as:

A Cristo prendieron en el huerto porque allí se estuvo quieto—They caught Christ in the garden [of Gethsemane] because he stood still there [he accepted his fate]. This ironic saying declaims that though Christ accepted his fate without a fight, the speaker intends to take the opposite course of action.

Tienes más fuerza que Dios con su poderío—You're stronger than God in all his might.

Este tío no da el brazo a torcer ni a Dios—lit: Not even God can twist this guy's arm; meaning: This person doesn't give in, not even to God.

The expression *Ni Dios* or *Ni Cristo*, means *nadie* (nobody), No-one/ Not even God/Not even Christ, and is used for example in a phrase such as: *Con este niño no puede ni Dios*—Not even God can cope with this boy.

In a picturesque, and perhaps stereotypical manner, the collective Spanish essence is often equated with the unharnessed will and tragi-comic enterprises of Don Quijote. Such an impression of Spanishness, or of a Spanish idealistic view of life, is incomplete, for Cervantes wrote not just about the emaciated, ascetic and idealistic adventurer Don Quijote, but about Quijote and his *escudero* (or squire/servant) Sancho Panza. Sancho Panza, the fat, uncultured, simple realist, whose feet, and even whose belly, are very much on the ground and who is in touch with reality in its most basic form. These two protagonists are almost impossible to separate in any discussion of Spanishness. Don Quijote does not exist without Sancho at his side and in many ways, these two elements—*quijotismo* (quixotism) and *sanchopancismo* (sanchopanzism)—form the essence of the Spanish way of being. In his essay *El Porvenir de España* (The Future of Spain), Unamuno refers to this notion when he affirms:

> Don Quijote and his squire Sancho are, while remaining distinct, united in a harmonious dualism—the eternal symbol of humanity in general and of our Spanish people in particular.[32]

The Spanish are a people who personify paradox and contradiction, who combine in their being the dichotomy of Quijote and Sancho: the dualisms of idealism and realism; the rational and the irrational; mysticism and the mundane, the religious and the profane.

The Sacred and the Profane

Though many of the above-mentioned contradictions are basic to the human condition itself, certain aspects of them seem to predominate in the Spanish outlook on life. This is perhaps noted most sharply in the Spanish attitude towards religion, and in particular that mixture of the religious and the profane that is observed, and most explicitly expressed in colloquial speech. Again, aspects of this can be observed in other cultures, but the sheer number and variety of these expressions used in Spanish is astounding, particularly so in Andalusia, where the people's natural spontaneity in the use of language means that the range of expressions is endless. This mixing of the sacred and the profane is thrown into greater relief when compared with the Anglo-Saxon world view, where the subject of religion is still, even today, treated with considerable respect, and perhaps somewhat puritanical and venerable deference, and where the crude and irreverent idioms used in Spanish slang and colloquial speech would often be considered offensive and probably blasphemous, even by those of a secular persuasion.

Many would find it surprising that from a country whose religious background and culture are steeped in catholic tradition, almost all proverbs and idioms relating to the Church or its ministers are of a negative inclination. As we saw earlier, such expressions can be fiercely anti-clerical, cynical and even sacrilegious. At the same time, they are intoned in a language that is full of colour, exotic imagination, humour, picaresque wit and crude metaphor. What is more, these coarse expressions are not the monopoly of an under-educated, marginalised few, but are commonly employed by people from all levels of society.

One such example of this, and, to foreign ears, often the most shocking, is the way the word *hostia* (the communion host) is used as a metaphor, mostly in a pejorative sense, or as an expletive, curse, or exclamatory tag word. As an illustration of the number and range of expressions employing the word *hostia*, we shall look at some of the most common below.

Perhaps the most offensive-sounding example of the use of the word 'host' in present-day popular speech is the much-encountered expression:

> *Me cago en la hostia*—lit: I shit on the host. This is often used to indicate irritation or misfortune/bad luck, etc., and means something like: God-damn!, Shit!, or as an equivalent of a four-letter word.

Another exclamatory expression, *¡Ahí va la hostia!* (lit: There goes the host!), is used to express surprise or astonishment and means: gosh, jeez, Good Heavens, bloody hell,etc. Other idioms expressing similar sentiments are:

> *¡Hostia divina!*—lit: Divine host!
> *¡Hostia puta!* —lit: Whore/prostitute host!
> *¡Hostia santa!* —lit: Sacred/holy host!

These exclamations, depending on the context, could also indicate indignation, much in the same way as: *¡Hostia!* or *¡Qué hostias!* (literally: What hosts!), and which mean something like Damn, or What the hell! Other common expressions include:

Mala hostia—lit: Bad host; but meaning: Bad tempered or bad mood, for example:

El está de mala hostia	He's in a foul mood
Tener mala hostia	To have a bad temper

Hostia by itself is often used as a metaphor to imply the pits/a pain in the arse/too much. Hence: *Anda, que eres la hostia*—Get off, you're a pain in the arse/you're too much.

Hostia could also mean a knock, smack, punch, blow. Thus:

Dar/Pegar una hostia	lit: To give/hit a host; meaning: To give/be asking for a smack, or punch.
Darse/Pegarse una hostia	To have a bad crash/smash in a car.
Hinchar/inflar a uno a hostias	lit: To inflate someone with hosts; but meaning: To give someone a beating.

There are other unexpected and surreal meanings, for example *hostia* can also be used to indicate speed:

Iba a toda hostia—lit: He was going at full host; meaning: full speed.
Iba echando hostias—lit: He was throwing hosts; meaning: He was going very fast.

Hostia is even used as a negation:

¡ . . . ni hostias!—meaning: No way!

Or the more colourful:

¡Hostias en vinagre!—lit: Hosts in vinegar/pickled hosts, but again meaning: No way!

Recently, I also heard the graphic expression where the host is referred to as if it were a slice of *chorizo* sausage:

Eres más basto que un bocadillo de hostias—You are coarser/more uncouth than a host sandwich.

It is also fascinating to discover what further analysis of colloquial speech and slang expressions tells us about the modern-day attitude towards religion in general, and in particular about the religious orders (priests, monks and nuns), and the Institution of the Church and the religious belief system. Later, in part two of this section, we shall be looking in some detail at the use of proverbs in the Golden Age, and will see that many of the scathing maxims and idioms on the subject of religion are still common currency today.

With respect to the men and women of the church, one often encounters critical, cynical or picaresque expressions such as:

Amor de monja y pedo de fraile, todo es aire—A nun's love and a friar's fart -it's all air!

El fraile en su convento, y bien adentro—This cautions that friars should be kept out of the way, securely locked inside their monasteries.

Fraile limosnero, pájaro de mal agüero—A mendicant friar is a bird of bad luck/a prophet of doom.

Al fraile y al cochino, no les enseñes el camino—Never show the way to a friar or a pig; meaning: Do not encourage a friar or a pig.

Si quieres tener un hijo pillo, métele a monaguillo—If you want a rogue for a son, make him an altar boy.

En la casa del cura, siempre jartura [hartura]—This is a sardonic Andalusian proverb protesting that: In the priest's house there's always a surfeit [of food].

Trabajar para el obispo—This Andalusian saying translates literally as: To work for the bishop; but means: A useless job.

Entre santo y santa, pared de cal y canto—lit: Between a male and female saint, a whitewashed wall; meaning: Two pious people of opposite sex should be kept well apart.

Los frailes en jubón, hombres son—Friars wearing doublets are men [nonetheless].

No digas nunca de este agua no he de beber, ni este cura no es mi padre.—Never say, of this water "I will not drink it", nor of this priest "he is not my father." (This is another piquant Andalusian saying.)

A striking aspect of Spanish popular speech, and one that is particularly relevant to the popular speech of *Andalucía*, is the added force that is lent to expressions, especially comparisons, by the juxtaposition of opposite symbols. Perfect examples of this are commonly used contrary expressions such as:

Está de puta madre—lit: It's a mother whore; but meaning: Fantastic.

This idiom is used to indicate that something or someone is superb, great, or excellent; for example in a phrase such as:

El vino está de puta madre—The wine is fantastic.

What strikes one most about this expression *está de puta madre*, is that it takes perhaps the most revered and idealized of all symbols in Spain, the mother, and juxtaposes this with one of the most derided, the prostitute. This use of opposites to indicate augmentation or uniqueness is something we shall return to later. But here, once more, it serves to underscore the inherent tension resulting from the interplay and intertwining of opposing characteristics in the language of Spanish popular speech. This can be seen yet again in the Andalusian expression:

Má[s] puta que Santa Rita—A bigger whore than St. Rita

where the name of the good and saintly Rita is invoked to call someone a prostitute.

And even to express purity or whiteness, you will come across such earthy, not to say crude, expressions as the Andalusian idiom:

Má[s] blanca que la teta [de] una monja—Whiter than a nun's nipple/tit.

Warnings about the hypocrisy and avarice of the religious orders are ever recurring in Spanish idioms and proverbs as we saw earlier. Particularly vivid are some of the following examples:

Más falso que un abad en oración—Falser than an abbot at prayer.

Parece que lo ha hecho la boca de un fraile—He seems to have been made in a friar's mouth. This Andalusian proverb refers to someone who is forever asking for things or favours, a practice associated with friars.

Beatas con devoción, largas tocas y el rabo ladrón.—Pious women with devotion [have] long headdresses and a thief's tail.

El rosario al cuello y el diablo en el cuerpo—Rosary around the neck and the devil in the body.

Cuando los médicos ayunan, lloran los curas.—When the doctor doesn't eat, the priest cries [this infers that when people are well and in good health, there are few funerals for which the priest can charge a fee].

Quien sirve a convento, sirve al viento—He/She who works in a convent, works for the wind [nothing/little remuneration].

In this context, on a visit to Andalusia, I overheard a gardener in Jerez jokingly offer the following proverbial advice to a friend:

Onde [Donde] hay beato, no guardes el jato [hato].—When a pious person is about, don't leave your bundle/belongings [because he will take it].

The institution of the Church and the religious belief system in general seem to be regarded with particular cynicism in Andalusia, where we come across such sayings as:

Si en el sexto no hay remisoria, ¿quién es el guapo que va a la gloria?—If for breaking the 6th [commandment] there is no remission, who is the lucky one that will reach heaven?

Por mí, que diga misa—lit: For me, he can say mass; but meaning: As far as I'm concerned, I don't give a damn.

Echar los kiries—lit: To throw up kyries, meaning: to vomit. This alludes to the prayer *Kyrie eleison* (Lord have mercy), which is said during mass.

No cantar el kirieleisón—lit: Not to sing the Kyrie eleison; meaning: Not to be ruled by anyone/Not to toe the line.

Among some of the most picaresque expressions employing religious allusions are the following:

Hacer el viacrucis—lit: To do the stations of the cross; but meaning: To go to bars/go on a pub crawl with friends.

Visitar los sagrarios—lit: To visit the tabernacles; meaning: To go to bars/go on a pub crawl. This expression refers to the Spanish custom on Maundy Thursday of visiting the tabernacles of different churches, which have been decorated in a spectacular fashion for the occasion.

Belén is another biblical reference, which literally means: Bethlehem, nativity scene, crib. However in popular speech, it often refers to other things. *Belén* can mean problems, disorder or gossip, as for example in the phrase: *No me vengas con belenes*—Don't come to me with problems; or *Meterse en belenes*; meaning: To get into a jam or fix. Other curious uses for the word, heard in Andalusia, are in contexts such as:

Llegar a Belén—lit: To arrive at Bethlehem/at the nativity crib; but meaning: To arrive home drunk on Christmas day, after spending the night on the tiles, or going on a pub crawl.

Tener un Belén—meaning: To have an illicit affair.

Estar en Belén con los pastores—lit: To be in Bethlehem with the shepherds; meaning: To be in another world, to be day dreaming.

Reference to religiosity itself is made directly in the expression: *mear agua bendita*—lit.: to pee holy water; but meaning to be a very religious person: *María mea agua bendita*—Mary pees holy water; meaning she is very religious. Holy water is again employed in the expression: *Echar agua bendita*—lit. To sprinkle with holy water; but meaning: To revive someone. This is often used in conjunction with a sports person, such as a footballer: *Le echaron agua bendita al jugador*—They revived the player.

The examples we have seen are just a few of the scores that exist and show how Spanish, and in particular Andalusian, popular speech is full of biblical and religious allusions, but which are turned on their head and used contrarily in a sceptical or scoffing tone. Examples of other such popular and colourful idioms are:

Como dijo Herodes, ¡te jodes!—As Herod said: fuck off!

Pasar las de Caín—lit: To suffer Cain's tribulations; but meaning: To go through hell.

Hay una Salomé que me ha quitado la cabeza—There's a Salome who has driven me out of my head.

Ser más basto que un rosario de melones—To be coarser than a rosary of melons.

A santo que no me agrada, ni Padrenuestro ni nada—To a saint I don't like, [I offer] neither an Our Father nor anything else.

Even for a common word like *enseguida,* which means: straight away/immediately, there are numerous versions with religious allusions:

En un decir Jesús/amén—In the time it takes to say Jesus/amen.

En un santiamén—In a holy amen.

En un credo/padrenuestro/Ave María—In a creed/an Our Father/an Ave Maria.

En menos que canta un gallo—In less time than the cock crows.

En menos que se santigua uno—In less time than it takes to cross oneself.

En menos que se persigna un cura loco—In less time than it takes a mad priest to make the sign of the cross.

To indicate distance there are several idioms which fall into the category of unpredictable or absurd humour. Most of these indicate a sense of remoteness as in: the back of beyond, the middle of nowhere:

Donde Cristo perdió el gorro/la alpargata/el mechero/las llaves.—Where Christ lost his cap/his sandal/his cigarette lighter/his keys.

Donde Cristo dio las tres voces—Where Christ shouted/yelled thrice.

Though the Spanish mix the contrasting elements of quixotism and sanchopanzism, they do not confuse or homogenize them. As in the vivid and telling expression *más puta que Santa Rita* (a bigger whore than St. Rita), the crude, the sacred and the profane are mixed in a comparison in which each element retains its independence. This is equally true of the many contradictory idioms such as:

Valiente cobarde—lit: Brave coward; but meaning: A real coward.

Bonita bestia—lit: Pretty beast; but meaning: A real beast.

Ser un vivalavirgen—lit: To be a long-live-the-virgin; but meaning: Someone with a devil-may-care, irresponsible attitude.

Ser [devoto] de la virgen del puño—lit: To be devoted to the Virgin of the fist; meaning: To be tight-fisted/mean.

Estar hecho la santísima mierda—To feel like the most holy shit.

Paradox and contradiction reign supreme here, since the Spanish dialectic is a binary dialectic, not a German, tenary, Hegelian dialectic. For the Spaniard, the thesis and antithesis are not mediated or resolved into a harmonious synthesis. The two contrasting elements are ever present in a constant struggle as to which one predominates. The Spaniard is in many ways a living representation of his unsystcmatic philosophy, of a contradictory, binary dialectic that not only does not resolve into a synthesis, but does not want to; paradox is of his essence.

A tradition within Spanish literature and religious thought that has had a great impact on the people and their life is that of the Spanish mysticism. The Spanish mystic is an idealist who is at the same time in touch with reality. St. Teresa of Avila and St John of the Cross may well have levitated in ecstatic contemplation, but most of the time they had their feet very firmly on the ground. When these mystics expressed their most pure and mystic love in language, they speak of God and their relationship to God in very human terms. The individual is always at the centre of the relationship. For both, their God is not a distant God who is simply up or out there, but very much "my" God, who is a friend and indeed a "lover" or "spouse", someone who is always at my side. God is spoken of as being found in the most mundane of places. For St Teresa, he is found *entre los pucheros*, among the pots and pans. And in the context of our discussion of popular speech, when comparing the prose and poetic language of the mystics to the language of *el pueblo*, the people, we often find that for the ordinary person, God is not only at our side, but He is expected to be "on our side" in the struggles and squabbles of everyday life.

This is observed in particular in the use of *maldiciones* (curses), and especially *maldiciones gitanas* (gypsy curses). An example of this is the one I heard being invoked some time ago by a gypsy who had been refused money, when she spat out: *Permita Dios que te tragues un paraguas y cuando esté en tu barriga se te abra* (May God permit that you swallow an umbrella and when it's in your stomach it opens out). It was not only the colour and spontaneity of the curse that made it so memorable, but in the context of this study, it is also the *Permita Dios* (May God permit). And this is typical of the way curses are used in Spanish, that God, not the devil, but God or Christ, as my friend and thus as someone who is naturally on my side, is exhorted to rain down all sorts of disasters and misfortune on the person who is my perceived enemy at the time.

Again, linking life with literature, this was also the attitude of young Lazarillo (in *El Lazarillo de Tormes*, the first picaresque novel, written in 1554). Poor Lazarillo, whose master, the cleric, kept on starvation rations, and who only ate a decent meal when there was a local burial and the dead person's family invited the priest and himself to the meal afterwards. Lazarillo tells how he *"deseaba y aun rogaba a Dios que cada día matase el suyo"*[33] (wished and even begged God to kill one of his own every day) so that he himself could keep body and soul together. God was obviously expected to be on his side, even if it meant killing other poor people so that his Lazarillo could survive.

The following are just a few examples of the scores of gypsy curses recorded over the last few years, in which God is invoked as a powerful force, friend and accomplice in order that the individual concerned may achieve an often grotesque caprice or hateful desire:

Que Dios te regale tres cosas en una semana: la cárcel, el hospital y el cementario—May God send you three things in one week: prison, hospital and the cemetery.

Permita Dios que Cristo te mande una sarna perruna por mucho tiempo—May God permit that Christ send you a mangy itch and that it last a long time.

Permita Dios que, si eres casado, tu mujer te ponga los cuernos.—May God permit that, if you are married, your wife gives you a pair of horns.

Permita Dios que malos cuervos te saquen los ojos—May God permit that evil crows pick out your eyes.

Permita Dios que los demonios te lleven en cuerpo y alma volando al infierno—May God permit that devils carry you body and soul to hell.

A striking exclamation I overheard when visiting a friend in an emergency ward of a hospital in Seville was from a woman who was clearly under great stress while waiting to see if her son would survive. After standing motionless for some time, she suddenly blurted out: *"Parece un sapo boca abajo, atado de pies y manos, como un Cristo aplastado. ¡Desde luego, Dios tiene un salero! Más guasa que el diablo."* (He looks like a toad upside down, tied by his hands and legs, like a squashed Christ. You know, God can be a real joker! Even worse than the devil.)

Spanish popular speech, like its literature down the centuries, is also full of black humour, *tremendismo*, exaggerated often macabre satire and tragi-comic expressions which fall within the picaresque tradition of *El Buscón Don Pablos* (The Swindler) by the seventeenth-century writer Francisco de Quevedo, and even in the twentieth-century as reflected in *La Familia de Pascual Duarte* by Camilo José Cela. Examples of this are such present-day idioms as:

¡Cómprate un muerto y llórale!—lit: Buy yourself a corpse and cry over it!; an exaggerated way of telling someone who is particularly heavy going to "Get lost!".

El muerto al hoyo, y el vivo, al bollo—The dead man to the hole, and the living to the bread roll.

Tener cara de viernes santo—lit: To have the face of Good Friday; meaning: To look awful.

Pareces un entierro de tercera—You look like a third class funeral, and meaning: You look so bored.

Me ha mirado un tuerto—lit: A one-eyed person has looked at me; but meaning: bad luck. This can be heard in such contexts as: *¡Qué temporada llevo! Parece que me ha mirado un tuerto*— What a time I'm having lately, with such a run of bad luck.

Such expressions belong to the country's tradition of black humour, and though at times politically incorrect, they form part of a long heritage of tragi-comedy and *esperpento*, or grotesque and macabre depictions. This even extends into Spanish art, for one only has to think of the fantastic representation of Goya's so-called black paintings and the etchings entitled *Los Disparates* (Follies), with their extraordinary claro-oscuro effects. In this way, we can see that Spanish popular speech reflects a picaresque and imaginative view of the world, which can be at once colourful and dark.

One of the most simple yet visually striking improvisations I heard recently was the imagery used by a young Andalusian woman who was complaining that she had diarrhea and was in some discomfort. Describing this she said: "*Se me ha puesto el culo como una flor*" (It's turned my backside into a flower). Apart from the fact that such ailments and treatments for problems in the body's nether regions (diarrhea, constipation, piles, the use of suppositories, etc.) are talked about quite normally in Spain, unlike some more reserved countries where such conditions seem just to be whispered about in doctor's surgeries, here the humour in the expression—the use of the image of a flower, a thing of beauty to describe something unpleasant—gave an immediate and spontaneous picture of the poor woman's predicament: her backside was stinging and as red as a flower in full bloom! Two other particularly compact and vivid Andalusian sayings are:

> *Dios nos crió hermanos, pero no primos*—lit: God created us brothers, but not cousins/idiots. This saying plays on the word *primo* which normally means cousin, but in colloquial speech can also mean an idiot/fool. Thus the saying's meaning is: One should show brotherly love, but not be taken for a ride/be stupid.

> *Al que es un alma de Dios, lo engañan tós*—A child of God is cheated by all.

This visual and humorous mode of expression and dramatic sense of language come into their own in *Andalucía*, where the language itself becomes liquescent, and where the exuberance of the people's inventiveness is inexhaustible. An inventiveness and richness of expression that has led a novelist of the stature of Gonzalo Torrente Ballester to declare:

> I come here [to Andalusia] to hear them speak, not as up in the north. The solution of the Spanish language lies in Anadalusia and this is not flattery. I am only sorry that I don't live here so as to learn it [the language].[34]

In this section we have endeavoured to offer a wider panorama of the Spanish conception of life, linking Spanish folklore—their way of being and seeing the world—with their way of speaking about it, with language, and in particular with the religious symbolism reflected in popular speech. Earlier, in our version of an old Spanish proverb we said: *Dime qué hablas y te diré quién eres*

(Tell me what you say and I'll tell you who you are) and what we have heard so far, we believe has shown us a people who delight in the use of opposites, mixing them, but not in a melting pot where all is dissolved into one homogenious whole, but in a *puchero*, or stew (elaborating on St Teresa's metaphor), like the Spanish *cocido*, chick pea stew, where the ingredients are cooked together, but often served separately. A *cocido* of paradoxes where the ingredients remain independent and retain their own value and substance. Where we find the dualisms of idealism and realism; mysticism and the mundane, the sublime and the earthy, the religious and the sacrilegious, but where the earthy, sanchopanzist and profane elements tend to predominate. A spontaneous, down-to-earth attitude to life, tinged with a hint of cynicism, as again we see exhibited in two such well-known sardonic sayings as.

> *Quien tiene din, tiene don*—Where there's money (*din— dinero*), there's deference (the title *don*).

> *Los hijos de mis hijas nietos son; los hijos de mis hijos sépalo Dios*—My daughters' children are my grandchildren; my sons' children, God only knows. An old Spanish adage which brings to mind the modern-day American saying: Mommy's baby, daddy's maybe.

* * * *

2. Popular Humanism and The Golden Age

The importance afforded to folk-wisdom by Spanish humanists is a consequence of their emphasis on human values and appreciations. A perception concisely expressed by the Sophist philosopher Protagoras, arguably the first humanist, credited with the lapidary phrase "man is the measure of all things"—a saying that has all the hallmarks of a perfect adage.

This section looks at how the pithy language of proverbial dicta mirrors the way life is perceived and felt by the ordinary man and woman in Golden Age Spain. More precisely, it examines the way in which proverbs recite the ideas and common beliefs about the institution of the Church and its ministers at this time of religious turmoil in Europe.

As Américo Castro asserts: "the Renaissance venerates popular culture as an object of reflection . . ."[35] For the humanists of the Golden Age, proverbs came to be regarded as linguistic gems, whose brilliance reflected the insights and condensed wisdom of *el pueblo*. They were seen as a manifestation of the popular philosophy of their users, of how and what the common man and woman thought and felt about the world in which they lived.

Among the Renaissance humanists in Spain, Pedro Vallés, Hernán Núñez and Juan de Mal Lara were the first major paroemiologists to endeavour to combine two seemingly disparate oral and literary currents: the popular and the cultured veins in language and wisdom. Juan de Mal Lara especially, as he stated in the Preambles to his *Philosophia Vulgar* (Popular Philosophy), endeavoured to confer the same dignity on popular Spanish proverbs as that afforded to the classical adages of antiquity, for, after all, many of these classical adages had been in popular oral use long before being recorded by renowned poets and philosophers. In the Preamble entitled "The Origin of Popular Philosophy", he equates the folk wisdom transmitted orally through the generations, with scientific knowledge and the philosophy enshrined in Greek axioms.[36] The book contained 1000 adages, which he glossed with great style and erudition, including anecdotes, stories, fables and jokes in his commentaries. It also offered much insight into folklore, customs, artisan practices, festivals, food, etc., and constitutes one of the most outstanding paroemiological reflexions that popular humanism has produced in Spain. It is this popular vein within Spanish humanism on which we shall focus our attention, particularly the inter-relationship between the Erasmian spirit of religious protest and the homespun wisdom reflected in the proverbial dicta of the age.

As the works of Vallés and Hernán Núñez reflect, during the first half of the sixteenth century the number of proverbs about the religious orders increased greatly in oral tradition. This was the case until around the middle of the 16th century when inquisitorial control began to censor written transmission of anticlerical dicta, for by and large, this is what they were. However, this did not prevent such ideas being disseminated orally, since the spoken word is clearly much more difficult to control than the written word. Almost all Spanish proverbs in circulation during the Golden Age relating to the Church and its ministers are of a negative inclination—fiercely critical, mockingly anti-clerical and cynical. This can be seen in the examples below, though much of their pungency and wit is lost in translation, especially as their rhythm and assonant rhyme often has to be forfeited:

O el fraile ha de ser ladrón o el ladrón ha de ser fraile—Either the friar is a thief, or the thief is a friar.[37]

Obispos y abriles los más ruines—Bishops and Aprils are treacherous. (The month of April is renowned for its unstable and often treacherous weather.)

Amor de monja y fuego de estopa y viento de culo, todo es uno—The love of a nun and fire of hemp and wind from the arse: it's all the same. This proverb, which first appeared in Santillana, is recorded by all the major paroemiologists of the Golden Age. A proverb with a similar sentiment is noted by Correas in his *Vocabulario de refranes ...* (Collection of Adages ...) of 1627 as: *Amor de monja y pedo de fraile todo es aire*—A nun's love and a friar's fart: it's all air.

This negative perception of the Church and its ministers was so widely held by ordinary people that many proverbs recorded suspicions, in very colourful and often earthy language, about the dangers of contact with ecclesiastics. For example: *Con putas ni frailes, ni camines ni andes* (Keep whores and friars at arm's length); *Guárdate de frailes, de infiernos y de cuernos* (Keep away from friars, hell and horns [cuckolds]); *Dios te guarde de la delantera de viuda y de la trasera de mula y de lado de un carro y del fraile, de todos cuatro* (May God protect you from four things: the front [breasts] of a widow, the hind of a mule, the sides of a cart, and a friar).

In this way, proverbs became the refuge in popular speech for religious protest and echo the traditional attack on ecclesiastical power waged in other parts of Europe. This is particularly obvious in proverbs such as: *Roma, Roma, la que a los locos doma y a los cuerdos no perdona* (Rome, Rome, the mad she tames and the sane she does not absolve); *Bula del Papa, ponla sobre la cabeza y págala de plata* (A papal bull: wear it on your head and pay for it in silver); *Piedra de iglesia, oro gotea* (A church stone drips gold); *Iglesia, o mar, o casa real, quien quiera medrar* (The church, or the sea, or royal patronage—for the man who wants to prosper). Of the approximately 250 proverbs recorded by Cervantes in his *Quijote*, only four are critical of the Church and ecclesiastics, managing somehow to escape the Inquisition's censorship. One of these is a shortened version of this proverb: *Iglesia o mar o casa real* (Book I, 39). Another pertinent one is: *Bien se está S. Pedro en Roma*—St Peter is well situated in Rome (II, 41, 53 and 59); here St. Peter refers to the Pope.

Criticism and disapproval of the religious, political and economic power of the institution of the Church, reflected in the above proverbs, was in turn extended to the hypocrisy of its ministers: their easy and privileged life-style, their avarice, lust and general debauchery. This is mirrored in the sardonic censure of such proverbs as:

"Hija María ¿con quién te quieres casar?" "Con el cura, madre, que no masa y tiene pan".—"Maria, child, whom do you want to marry?" "The priest, mother, who doesn't knead but always has bread".

El abad, de lo que canta yanta—The abbot eats where he sings for his meat. This proverb specifically refers to the perceived easy life enjoyed by ecclesiastics, it is another of the anti-clerical maxims recorded by Cervantes in *Quijote* (II, 60 and 71).

Monjas y frailes para dar echan las llaves; para tomar, ábrenlas de par en par—Nuns and friars when it comes to giving they lock the door, when it comes to taking they throw it wide open.

El abad que no tiene hijos es que le faltan los argamandijos—If an abbot doesn't have children, it's because he doesn't have the tackle [equipment].

Por las piernas del vicario sube la moza al campanario—By climbing up the vicar's legs the maiden reaches the bell tower.

Niña, si quieres ventura, tómale clérigo que dura—Girl, if you want fortune, take a cleric who'll last. This highlights the security and good life afforded by the lasting nature of a priest's sexual and economic potency. As we shall see later when looking at the relationship between proverbs and *cantares* (popular songs and lyric poems originally transmitted orally), Correas glossed this proverb in the form of a satirical poem.

To find a proverb or expression that is of a positive nature on this subject is like looking for a needle in a haystack. The proverbs mentioned above are only a few of the many which take a swipe at the vanity, avarice, vices and general lack of piety and public virtue exhibited by the religious orders, overagainst the sanctity, poverty and morality they preached. In this way, such adages helped sabotage the established religious order by subjecting it to censure in a *vulgar* tongue. For the unpolished stricture vented in irreverent criticism, ridicule and disparaging epithets has a more vital hold on the public imagination. The invective and wit of such a pithy language of protest abets the promulgation of its message, and hence its clout. The *vulgar* tongue thus becomes a very sharp and penetrating instrument with which to attack smugness, cant and ecclesiastical corruption.

It was said, regarding the Reformation, that Erasmus laid the egg that Luther went on to hatch. In Spain religious protest was promulgated by the Erasmian paroemiologists, whose analyses of popular proverbs, both in prose and verse, echo the spirit of protest and demand for reform taking place in northern Europe. But whereas the dissent in northern climes became increasingly more fierce and extreme, and eventually led to the Protestant schism, in Spain—in the manner of Erasmus's less violent demand for moderate reform—popular criticism and disapproval of the corruption and vices of the Roman church remained, for the most part, a protest from within.

Throughout the sixteenth and seventeenth century compilations and glosses of proverbs flourished, such that by the second half of the 17TH century *el refranero español*, the main body of Spanish proverbs, was well established. This is clearly reflected in the fact that from the 750 proverbs collected by the Marquis of Santillana in *Refranes que dicen las viejas* ... (Sayings Used by Old Women ...) in the first half of the fifteenth century, the number rises to some 18,000 compiled and glossed by Correas in 1627, in his *Vocabulario de refranes y frases proverbiales* ... (Collection of Adages and Proverbial Phrases ...), though this latter was not published until the beginning of the twentieth century.

With the dawning of the Renaissance in Spain at the beginning of the sixteenth century, an optimistic, outgoing and more receptive period was ushered in. International ideas and aesthetic currents from other European countries were embraced with enthusiasm and had great resonance throughout the country. This period also saw the arrival in the Peninsula of the Habsburg King, Charles V (Holy Roman Emperor from 1519), an event which aided the change in the climate of ideas. However, in Spain these Renaissance tendencies and the new Copernican vision of the individual and his place in the universe were to fuse with deep-rooted national values and an entrenched Hispanic religious spirit. For this reason Erasmian Christian humanism had a greater impact on society as a whole than the more pagan, or amoral and anarchic currents experienced in Italy. The influence of the Italian Renaissance was particularly noticeable in the arts, and more especially in the sphere of poetry, where Garcilaso de la Vega was hailed as the Spanish Renaissance poet *par excellence*, and who more than anyone else embodied the ideal of the cortesan. Yet in literature and ideas many of the most outstanding writers, particularly during the reign of Felipe II, were men and women of the church, such as: Fray Luis of León, Fray Luis of Granada, and especially ascetic and mystical writers like St. Teresa of Avila and St. John of the Cross. In this respect, the Spanish experience had more in common with the pietistic tendencies of the northern Renaissance, where it soon became entangled with the Reformation.

In fact, the flame of humanism in Spain was lit in the early 1500s with the reformist spirit engendered by Cardinal Cisneros, who founded the University of Alcalá in order to foster religious scholarship and biblical studies, as opposed to scholastic philosophy. Classical languages were taught with the purpose of applying them to theological ends, and one of the most important consequences of this was the production of the Polyglot Bible of 1514, written in Chaldean, Hebrew, Greek and Latin.

In this way, the Christian humanism of Erasmus was readily embraced in Spain, since the ideological ground had already been prepared by the upsurge in popular, emotive pietism which meant that Erasmian ideas could germinate more easily. Spanish scholars such as Luis Vives, Alfonso and Juan Valdés corresponded with Erasmus. Vives was the most renowned Spanish thinker of the

Erasmian movement, though partly due to his Jewish roots, he became more a citizen of Europe than of Spain. In fact, Erasmians at this time counted high officials of the Inquisition among their numbers. Surprisingly, perhaps, the ideas of Eramsus had an official protector in Spain in the person of the Inquisior-General himself, Alonso Manrique, Archbishop of Seville, who was a great defender of the Dutch scholar against his detractors. The first of Erasmus's works to be translated into Spanish was *Querela Pacis*, which was translated in 1520 by the Inquisitor López de Cortegana. This was followed in 1526 by the *Enchiridion*, which, incredible though it may seem now, was dedicated to the Inquisitor-General himself, and which was so popular that in the space of four years eight editions of the book had been printed. It contained the famous maxim *monachatus non est pietas* (piety does not reside in a monk's cowl; in Spanish: *el hábito no hace al monje*), and criticized the religious orders for their hypocrisy, avarice and vanity; sentiments which, as we have seen, were echoed in many Spanish proverbs of the time. Among other pertinent Golden-Age sayings in this vein are:

Debajo del buen sayo está el hombre malo—Under a good smock/cowl resides a bad man. Juan de Mal Lara glosses this proverb remarking that one cannot deduce that a person is good simply because he dresses in white or dresses well. To prove this he quotes the proverb: *Debajo lo blanco está el diablo*—Under a white garment resides the devil, and reinforces this by quoting Erasmus's adage: *El hábito no hace al monje.*

Diezma a la iglesia, aunque no quede pelleja—Tithes to the church, though you're just skin [and bone].

Si quieres un día bueno, hazte la barba; un mes bueno, mata puerco; un año bueno, cásate; un siempre bueno, hazte clérigo—If you want a good day, trim your beard; a good month, slaughter a pig; a good year, get married; a good life forever, become a cleric.

Ni por lumbre a casa del cura va la moza segura—Not even when calling at the priest's house for coal can a young girl feel safe.

Monjas y frailes, putas y pajes, todos vienen de grandes linajes— Nuns and friars, whores and pages, are all of noble lineage. In his gloss of this proverb, Correas castigates the vainglory and pretentiousness displayed by members of these professions.

One of the main differences between the *Adages* of Erasmus and the works of the Spanish paroemiologists of the Golden Age is that the latter, while acknowledging the significance and human values bequeathed in the adages of the classical world, paid special attention to the insights and popular humanism engraved in the *refranes* they recorded. In the Prologue of *Libro de refranes* (Book of Proverbs) by Mosén Pedro Vallés, published 1549, the author emphasizes the cross-current of influence in this work, reminding the reader that Erasmus took his *Adages* "from illustrious Greek and Latin authors, recording them in Latin and citing their origin. I compiled mine from Spanish oral tradition, taking them from here and there". Valles's *Libro de refranes* contains over 4000 adages, all listed systematically in alphabetical order— unlike Erasmus's *Adages*, which was purposely not given a systematic format, either as regards subject-matter or alphabetical listing, since the Dutch humanist preferred a more random approach. But within the Erasmian spirit censuring ecclesiastical excesses, Vallés includes around 100 proverbs of a marked anti-clerical nature, such as: *Quien a Roma buen bolsín llevó, vino abad o obispo* (Take a rich purse to Rome and return an abbot or bishop); *Roma, que sus manos tuerce quien en ella envejece* (Rome, who corrupts the hand of those who grow old there); *Teólogo, ancho de conciencia y angosto de bolsa* (Theologian: loose of conscience and tight of purse); *Sin clérigo y sin palomar tendrás limpio tu hogar* (Without a cleric and a pigeon loft, you'll have a clean home).

The death of Erasmus in 1536 was followed two years later by the demise of the Inquisitor-General, Alonso Manrique, the patron of Erasmian ideas in Spain, thus bringing to an end direct inside influence with the Inquisition. As Marcel Bataillon attests in his seminal work on the subject, *Erasme et l'Espagne*, the heterodoxies of the Dutch humanist now began to be attacked with greater zeal, and his works and those of his followers were banned as an incitement to protestantism.[38] They were eventually placed on the 1559 Index of prohibited books; however, by this time these ideas had already been disseminated and attitudes influenced.

As is clear from the above, in contrast to the first half of the 16TH century, the second half, coinciding with the reign of Felipe II, issued in a period of grave religious zeal and catholic reform. As a consequence of the Reformation, Europe was now divided into two halves: Catholics and Protestants. The negative effect of all this in Spain was that the open-minded attitude of the first half of the century gave way to an upsurge in anti-intellectual religious fervour. Spain became a champion of catholic ideals and a militant defender of Tridentine decrees. Unorthodox ideas were treated with great suspicion, national values, both political and religious, were asserted, and eventually a counter-attack was instigated, whereby dissemination of heterodox ideas was controlled and persecuted by the Inquisition.

Hernán Núñez's collection, *Refranes y proverbios* (Adages and Proverbs), published in 1555—a few years before the 1559 Index—managed to escape the Inquisition's interdiction. It contained 8000 proverbs, of which some 200 attacked ecclesiastical corruption of one sort or another. Thus we can see that in the space of 6 years, between the publication of the works of Vallés and Núñez, the number of anticlerical proverbs recorded had doubled. Núñez's work was the most anticlerical yet published, and this at a time when inquisitorial control was beginning to bite. This collection, in fact, marks the dividing line between writers who enjoyed the freedom to criticize ecclesiastical excesses, and those who came after, whose work was considerably circumscribed, for after this date the number of recorded proverbs about the Church and its ministers would diminish notably. Although Núñez was a Hellenist, Professor of Greek at Salamanca, his book followed the line taken by Vallés, documenting popular proverbial dicta. Núñez's collection is particularly colourful and underscores the graphic speech of the *vulgar* tongue in such adages as:

Ni amistad con fraile, ni con monja que ladre—Never befriend a friar, or a nun who barks.

Sin manceba ningún dómino, ni sin hideputa canónigo—No dominie without a mistress, no canon without a bastard child.

El padre vicario deja la misa y vase al jarro—The vicar leaves the mass and goes to the pitcher.

El abad de la Madalena, si bien come, mejor cena—The Abbot of Magdalen [Abbey] lunches well and dines better.

Amor de ramera, halago de perro, amistad de fraile, convite de mesonero no puede ser que no te cueste dinero—A whore's love, a dog's affection, a friar's friendship, an innkeeper's treat, are never free.

El abad y el gorrión dos aves malas son—The abbot and the sparrow are two evil birds. This curious adage designating the humble sparrow as evil is thought to refer to the way the bird was regarded in a largely agricultural society, where the sparrow was renowned for stealing grains of wheat and other costly seeds. The proverb was also recorded in *décima* form [a stanza of ten octosyllabic lines in full rhyme] by the paroemiologist Sebastián de Horozco in his *Teatro universal de proverbios* (Universal Theatre of Proverbs), collected between 1558-80. Horozco's *décima* gloss runs:

El gorrión y el abad	The sparrow and the abbot
nunca siembran pero cogen	Never sow, they only reap,
y en caso de humanidad	And when it comes to humanity,
tienen grande habilidad	They have great ability
y adonde pueden se acogen.	In getting what they seek.
Así que no sin razón	Thus the advice is quite sound
dijo de ellos el refrán	Which in the proverb is found:
que el abad y el gorrión	The abbot and the sparrow
dos muy malas aves son	Are two most evil birds
adondequiera que están.	Wherever they are found.

A similar proverb recorded later by Correas is:

Gorriones, frailes y abades, tres malas aves—Sparrows, friars and abbots are three evil birds.

The censure and disparagement of ecclesiastics mirrored in popular speech was not only a result of their vices and moral degeneracy. Nuñez's *Refranes y proverbios* shows that there was also much resentment and hostility towards them due to their activity as merciless collectors of tithes; taxes that many small-holders found crippling. An ironic proverb reflecting this animus is: *"Tarde venís, don fraile". "Pues que recaudo, no vengo tarde"* ("You're late, friar". "It's never too late to collect"). This antipathy, when allied to that caused by the avarice and abuses linked to their rapacious soliciting of alms in the name of God (when in reality most went straight into their own pockets) was also recorded by Núñez in such proverbs as: *Fraile que pide por Dios, pide para dos* (A friar collecting for God's due, collects for two); *Fraile que su regla guarda, toma de todos y no da nada* (The friar who follows the rules of his order, takes from all and gives to none).

Juan de Mal Lara was a humanist in the Erasmian mold, but one who, at the same time, had great interest in national folk knowledge. He was imprisoned in 1561 on suspicion of writing defamatory verses about the institution of the Church in Seville, although he was later found not guilty and released. However inquisitorial control was now at its most severe, and as a consequence Mal Lara was forced to remove the name of Erasmus from the manuscript of *Philosophia Vulgar* (Popular Philosophy), where it was originally cited some 200 times. When the book was eventually published in 1568, the major part of his collection of proverbs on the Church and its ministers was suppressed, thus the book does not project the anticlericalism seen in Hernán Núñez. Further, in Mal Lara's case, when he glosses a 'sensitive' proverb, the commentary does not censure the institution of the Church and its ministers as such, rather it very skillfully maneuvers itself round the bends of ecclesiastical control by taking the moral high ground, criticizing bad habits and poor Christian practice in general, and underscoring that which is righteous overagainst the failings that are all too common. In this way, the author had to exercise considerable self-censorship over his work. Further, the *Pragmática*, or Censorship Law, of 1558 meant that any book in Spanish had to be submitted to the scrutiny of the Inquisition's censors prior to publication, and *Philosophia Vulgar* was in their hands for some two years. In fact Mal Lara had originally wanted to gloss 10,000 proverbs, but only 1000 of these finally appeared in the book, and of these only 35 relate to clerics. One of these is: *Los diezmos de Dios, de tres blancas sisar dos* (Tithes for God: of three coins, pocket two). This proverb, which in itself is a clear criticism of ecclesiastical greed, and mirrors the hostility felt towards religious levies, escapes the black pen of the Inquisition because of the author's adroitness in providing a sanitized gloss. This he does by commenting that it is the obligation of all good Christians to give to the church, as decreed in the Gospel: "Render therefore unto Caesar the things which be Caesar's, and unto God the things which be God's." He then criticizes those who instead of giving to

God that which is ordained, use trickery and cheat, and "out of three coins, they pocket two", and instead of giving a full sack of wheat, they double-cross by mixing one part wheat with two parts earth. Thus they do not benefit from the sanctity to be gained in giving the church what is its due. Similar sophistry or verbal artifice is offered in his glosses of other proverbs such as: *Lo que no lleva Cristo, lleva el fisco* (If Christ doesn't take it, the tax man will); *Quien tiene pie de altar come pan sin amasar* (He who has a foot on the altar step, eats bread without kneading); *El lobo harto de carne métese fraile* (The wolf sated with meat becomes a friar).

However, of the 35 anticlerical proverbs mentioned by Mal Lara, the majority do not make specific mention of the religious orders as such, and his glosses confine themselves to offering righteous advice or moral admonitions of improper Christian action, as seen for example in: *Rogar al santo hasta pasar el tranco* (Pray with all your might till danger's out of sight); *Palabras de santo y uñas de gato* (Words of a saint and claws of a cat); *Romería de cerca, mucho vino y poca cera* (A pilgrimage taking place: much wine and little candle wax).

In the Preambles to his *Philosophia Vulgar*, Mal Lara makes special reference to the forced self-censorship which resulted in his sanitized collection of popular proverbs. It appears that he was left with little option but to take good regard of the Inquisition's rule that nothing offensive should be said about the Church and its ministers, as well as the order given by the King, Felipe II, that *"no se digan ni canten cosas sucias"* (nothing dirty should be said or sung about). Among the types of proverbs he mentions having excluded are those which are dirty, dishonest, blasphemous, lascivious and "that bite friars, clerics and nuns by being scandalous and giving the impression of having been engendered in the permissiveness of Germany, and which are dangerous for these times."[39]

As indicated earlier, the most extensive work of paroemiology of the era was Gonzalo Correas's tome compiled around 1627, which contained 18,000 adages and which was given the delightful title: *Vocabulario de refranes y frases proverbiales y otras fórmulas comunes de la lengua castellana en que van todos los impresos antes y otra gran copia que juntó el Maestro* (Collection of adages and proverbial phrases and other common forms of the Spanish language, including all those previously published and another considerable number added by the author).After this date, the body of Spanish proverbs hardly changed until the mid-nineteenth century, when the writings of the renowned folklorist Fernán Caballero contributed to the revival of interest in the country's folk-wisdom and regenerated the treasure-trove of Spanish adages.[40] Correas's *Vocabulario* contains the main body of proverbial dicta on the subject of ecclesiastics in Spanish. These amount to some 450 anticlerical maxims, a figure which highlights the importance of the Church and the religious orders in Spanish life at the time. Priests, friars, abbots, canons, nuns, bishops etc., had an all-pervading influence on society, and the *Vocabulario* criticizes their spiritual and economic power, privileged lifestyle, lust, and hypocrisy, as seen in the disparity between what they preached and how they lived. Reproof engraved in such emblematic proverbs as:

Líbrete Dios del delito contra las tres santas: Inquisición, Cruzada y Hermandad—God preserve you from sinning against the holy trinity: the Inquisition, the Crusade and the Brotherhood.

Bulda no, que sacan prendas—A papal bull no: you'll lose your shirt.

Dejar hambre y frío por amor de Dios—Leave behind hunger and cold, for love of God!

La hacienda del abad, cantando viene y chiflando se va—The Abbot's wealth: singing it comes and chortling it goes [easy come, easy go].

Anda el fraile con mesura, cada noche con la suya—Each night the friar must satisfy his desire.

Because this work remained unpublished until the twentieth century, such biting proverbs escaped the Inquisition's erasure and were thereby preserved for posterity. These 450 pithy sayings are able to give a heightened sense of history; a palpable appreciation of the spirit of the time. For they recite the popular nature of religious protest in Golden Age Spain, reflecting more graphically than any history text book the way ecclesiastical life was perceived by the ordinary person. From the 100 anticlerical maxims recorded by Vallés in 1549 to the 450 glossed by Correas in 1627, they chronicle the groundswell of popular ideas, and echo the complaints and demand for reform resonating in the intellectual corridors of Europe. They also stand as testimony to the way proverbial dicta helped subvert the established order by subjecting it to censure and ridicule in a *vulgar* tongue. A tongue that could not be silenced despite the fear generated by zealous authoritarian institutions against which no criticism could be uttered, as illustrated most vividly in the cautionary adage in circulation at the time:

Del Papa, del Rey y de la Inquisición, chitón, chitón
Of the Pope, the King and the Inquisition, shush, shush!

V

Spanish Literature and Folk Wisdom

~~~~

Oral Tradition and Literary Sources

Myth, fable, legend and history intertwine in the proverb, thus it is said that behind every adage lies a tale. And when this tale has been forgotten, lost in the mist of time, another tale is often invented to fit the proverb. As Correas says in his *Vocabulario de refranes* when recounting the tale of the hungry fox (an adaptation of the Aesopic fox and grapes fable), "*de cuentos fingidos se hacen refranes y de refranes se hacen o fingen cuentos.*" (from invented stories proverbs are made and from proverbs, stories are invented). Many Spanish proverbs have a direct link with ancient fables, others with rhymes, tales, tall stories, satirical verses, ballads, *letrillas*, and other literary works. There are also examples where the theme of a work, usually a poem or a play of the Golden Age, is condensed into either a refrain or a title which encapsulates the whole, and which thereafter achieves such popular acclaim that it is dignified with the status of a proverb. The *paremiólogos*, or compilers of proverbs, of the Golden Age accentuate the interrelation between the proverb, oral tradition and literature, since the proverb can be encountered in all literary currents in Spain and, as said earlier, in it the popular and cultured strains of language converge. Of course, this in itself would constitute an enormous area of study and one that would call for a volume in its own right. However, here, in this overview of the way the threads of the various literary genres and proverbs interweave, we are only able to take a brief look at the main currents of influence.

Ancient Fables

The following are examples of some of the most well-known ancient fables whose morals have, through the ages, become engraved in the Spanish language as popular adages:

No hagas las cuentas de la lechera—lit: Don't do your sums as the milkmaid does them; meaning: Don't count your chickens (before they are hatched). This Spanish proverbial phrase alludes to the Aesopic fable of the Milkmaid and her Pail, a story whose details vary from country to country and with the narrator. The fable was popularized in Spain in the eighteenth century by Samaniego in his *Fábulas morales*, a collection of 136 moral tales. The fable recounts how a milkmaid went off to market early in the morning with a pail of milk on her head, and as she walked along, she began to day-dream about what she could do with the money she received for the milk. Her plan was first of all to buy a large basket of eggs, which she could incubate so that they would soon produce one hundred little chicks. She could then sell the chicks and with the money buy a little pig. She would feed the pig well to fatten him up and then take him to market. With the money she received for the pig she could buy a cow and a little calf. The idea delighted her so much that she jumped with joy, whereupon the pail fell from her head and the milk spilt all over the ground. Thus all her dreams were in vain and the only thing she could look forward to was a scolding when she returned home empty handed.

[No matar] la gallina del huevo de oro—Don't kill the hen/ goose that lays the golden egg. This alludes to the Aesopic fable of the same name. In Spanish the animal depicted is a hen, whereas in English it is a goose. The fable tells of the farmer who, looking at his hen's nest one morning to see if it had laid an egg, finds to his amazement not an ordinary egg but one of solid gold. This he immediately takes back to his house to show

his wife. The hen continues to lay a golden egg every day, but as the farmer grows rich he also grows greedy. One day he has the idea that if he killed the hen he could possess all her treasure at once. He therefore decides to cut her open. Once the dreadful deed is done, he discovers that there is nothing inside the hen.

El perro del hortelano is another Aesopic fable evoked in the saying recorded by Santillana as: *el perro del hortelano, ni come las berzas ni las deja comer*—lit.: The gardner's dog neither eats cabbage nor lets others eat it. This refers to a person who has no desire to do something, but doesn't want anyone else to do it either, and in English it is usually translated at: A dog in a manger. [*Refranes que dicen las viejas*, 264; *Celestina*, Act VII, 162; Lope de Vega, *El perro del hortelano*, Act II, Sc.XXX.]

Local Tales

The tales below are examples of stories and anecdotes recounted by Mal Lara and other writers of the Golden Age in order to gloss a particular proverb:

A la mujer y a la picaza, lo que vieres en la plaza—lit.: Of a woman and a magpie, what you see in the market-place; meaning: A woman, like a magpie, repeats or mimics what she has heard others say. This misogynistic proverb suggests that women, like magpies, are unable to keep secrets. Mal Lara recounts a story which, he says, is appropriate to the meaning. This tells of a man who wanted to know if his wife could keep a secret. On going to bed one night, he decides to hide an egg under his pillow. Just as the man and his wife are about to go off to sleep, he suddenly seems unsettled and appears to have difficulty in breathing. When his wife asks him what is wrong, he replies that he can't tell a soul in case his misfortune were to become the subject of local gossip. After hearing his wife swear solemnly to keep his secret, the man tells her that he has given birth to an egg. As soon as she gets up in the morning, despite her promise, she calls on her neighbour and tells her how her husband has given birth to two eggs; the neighbour in turn increases the number to three when she recounts the story to someone else. By nightfall the number of eggs the man has apparently given birth to is up to a total of 40.

The next day, when the husband passes through the marketplace, someone hits him over the head with 40 eggs and tells him to go to the hen-house. Thus the man learns that his wife is unable to keep a secret.

After recounting the story, Mal Lara remarks on its misogyny, saying that there is no reason why in such things all the blame should be put on women, since most men have the same failing. Thus, he contends, it is much better to be ruled by the old maxim: *No fiar de persona alguna lo que quieres tener secreto*; do not confide in anyone about something you want to keep secret.

Más vale a quien Dios ayuda, que quien mucho madruga — It's better to have the help of God than be an early riser.

Mal Lara glosses this by telling the tale of a very diligent *panadera* (woman baker) who every day, while her lazy husband was still in bed asleep, would rise at the crack of dawn in order to prepare the dough for the bakery. One day when the *panadera* was scolding her husband for his laziness, a thief, who was fleeing over the rooftops, threw a bag of money through an open window so that he would not be caught with it on his person, and luckily it landed on the husband's bed. When the man saw this stroke of luck, he called out to his wife with glee saying, you see "*Más puede Dios ayudar que velar y trasnochar y madrugar y todo lo que vos andáis de aquí para allá*" — "God can do more for you than all the staying up late, working through the night, getting up early and the running around you do". [The proverb was also recorded in *Refranes que dicen las viejas*, 430; *Celestina*, Act VIII, 176; and *Quijote*, II, 34.] Mal Lara then refers to the Latin adage: *Dormientis rete trahit* (The net of the one who sleeps catches fish), in order to support his idea, pointing to the fact that, while fishermen go off to sleep in their boats, fish swim into their nets. He further tells how Timothy, the daring Athenian Captain, was said to have won more battles because he had luck on his side than for being a valiant fighter. Even in his portrait he was depicted as sleeping while luck 'in its great nets' won him cities and castles.

Juan de Timoneda, the sixteenth-century author of *patrañas*, or short stories, is another writer who glosses proverbs by recounting tales. One of his collections, entitled *El Sobremesa y alivio de caminantes* (After-dinner stories for the relief of travellers), published in 1563, contains 'affable and delightful sayings, heroic tales and a lot of didactic maxims.' Few of these stories are entirely his own, since many originated in the works of Boccaccio, Bandello and Morlini, among others.

One of Timoneda's after-dinner stories, tale number 58, entitled *Por qué se dijo: A buen capellán, mejor sacristán* (Why we say: To a good chaplain, a better sacristan), is an example of a story serving to explain the origin of a proverb.

This tells of how one day a chaplain was eating roast pigeon in a small village inn, when a traveller entered and asked if he could share his meal, for which he would, of course, pay his part. As the chaplain refused, the traveller had to make do with dry bread, and afterwards said: "I should tell you Reverend, that between you with the taste and me with the smell, we have eaten the pigeon together, although you didn't want to." To which the chaplain replied: "If that is the case, then I want you to pay your share of the pigeon". After some discussion, the local sacristan was brought in to decide on the question of payment. The sacristan asked the chaplain how much he had paid for the pigeon. "Half a *real*" (a Spanish coin) was the reply. The sacristan then told the traveller to give him *un cuartillo* (a quarter of a *real*). He took the coin and tapped the table with it, saying, "Reverend, this sound is your payment, just as the smell of the pigeon was the traveller's meal." At which a lodger at the inn said ironically: *A buen capellán, mejor sacristán.* [If the chaplain is good/astute, the sacristan is better/even more so.]

Correas later, in 1624, in his *Vocabulario de refranes*, records this proverb and glosses it recounting the same tale. The play on the chaplain/sacristan theme is repeated in a proverb glossed some 50 years earlier by Sebastián de Horozco in his *Teatro Universal de Proverbios*, but here to the contrary sense, i.e. *A mal capellán, mal sacristán* (To a bad chaplain, a worse sacristan), criticizing both the chaplain and the sacristan for their negligence in the way they carry out their duties. This is shown below, alongside an English translation which closely follows the text, though not the Spanish rhyming pattern:

Un bueno y otro mejor	One good and the other better
hacen gentil armonía	Produce gentle harmony,

por este mismo tenor	Being of the same condition,
un ruin con otro peor	One vile, the other worse
harán igual compañía.	They will form a perfect partnership.
De esta forma cantarán	In this way they will sing
un canto que sea unísono,	A song in unison,
así que a mal capellán	So that with a bad chaplain goes
otro peor sacristán	A worse sacristan,
que responda al mismo tono.	Who will respond in the same tone.

Horozco also mentions other versions of this proverb, again in *décima* verse form, e.g. *A mal abad, mal monacillo* (To a bad abbot, a bad altar boy); and *Como canta el abad, así responde el sacristán* (As the abbot sings, the sacristan replies [in the same tone]).

Another example of Timoneda's tales which purports to show the origin of a well-known proverb is tale number 59: *Por qué se dijo: nunca más perro al molino* (lit.: Why we say: never again the dog to the mill; meaning: Never again!). This is a story about a blind man who hid some money at the foot of a tree which stood on the land of a very rich farmer. One day he went to check that his money was still there and found it was missing. Whereupon he went to see the farmer, feigning to ask him for advice, saying: "I have a certain amount of money hidden away in a safe place, and now I have another lot of money and am undecided whether to hide it in the same place, or look for another." To which the farmer replied that if the place was so safe, he could see no reason for the blind man to seek another hiding place. "In that case," replied the blind man, "I'll leave it where it is." After the blind man had left, the farmer hurried along to the tree and replaced the money he had taken earlier, so as to reassure the blind man that his money was safe, but with the intention of returning later to steal both lots of money. The blind man then went to the tree and removed his money which he had almost given up as lost, declaring: *Nunca más perro al molino*, (Never again!). However, Timoneda's tale clearly does not explain the origin of this saying, rather the author used it as the inspirational kernel around which he could build his story. In fact, legend has it that the saying originated when a mischievous dog ran into a local mill and was beaten by the owner to teach it a lesson—never to return. [The proverb appears in *Celestina*, Act II, 99.]

The Sevillian writer, Juan de Arguijo (1560-1623), the author of a collection of stories that remained unpublished until 1902, sometimes used proverbs to encapsulate the moral of anecdotes and tales. One of the best-known of these is the adage:

Más vale maña que fuerza—Dexterity is better than strength/force. Recounting the anecdote behind this proverb, Arguijo tells how a wise man, who was hearing mass, suddenly felt someone tugging vigorously at his purse, in an attempt to remove it from his inside pocket. However the purse could not be dislodged, and the wise man turned to the thief and said: «*Señor hidalgo, ese negocio más se ha de hacer con maña que con fuerza.*» (Sir, this sort of business calls for dexterity rather than force.)

In Correas' extensive collection of proverbs there are also many summaries of stories, anecdotes or happenings which serve to highlight the origin of particular adages. The stories are condensed into the space of two or three lines either because the tale was so well known, or because the maxim itself was good summary of the tale, and needed little explanation. This was the case with:

El cura de Cantaracillo primero fue toro, después novillo— The priest of Cantaracillo at first was a bull, afterwards a bullock. Correas glosses this with a succinct anecdote telling how the priest was cut down to size. He relates that a priest from the village of Cantaracillo, near Olmedo, was a 'bull' in pressing his love for a young girl. However, one day he was caught by the girl's brother, who promptly castrated him.

Further examples of the way names of renowned or colourful people, usually from local areas, have been eternalized in proverbial language and slang can be seen in Section VII of the book, under the heading Names of People and Places in Popular Sayings.

As we have seen, there is a two-way current of influence between proverbs and stories: sometimes proverbs give rise to tales by serving as the nucleus or inspirational seed around which the story germinates; at other times the moral of a tale is condensed into a proverbial maxim. We have also had a glimpse of the way authors such as Horozco gloss adages in the form of lyric poems. The relationship between proverbs and *cantares* (different types of popular songs, or lyric poems, originally transmitted orally with musical accompaniment) is evidenced in the works of Golden Age authors such as Mal Lara, Horozco, Correas and Hernán Núñez. The latter, in particular, in his collection *Refranes o proverbios* (Adages or Proverbs) records a large number of *cantares*. M. Frenk Alatorre, in his modern study *Refranes cantados y cantares proverbializados* (Sung Adages and Proverbialized *Cantares*), refers to the way, from the Middle Ages onwards, lines became detached from *coplas* (popular poems or songs) and, over time, came to be used in the Spanish language as proverbial phrases. He also highlights numerous examples of *cantares* which were adages commented or developed in verse form, and which often incorporated a pithy moral in their refrain.[41] In this way, many proverbs had a musical ring and memorable rhyme, though this is often lost in translation; for example: *Pan y vino anda camino, que no mozo garrido* (Bread and wine help the job along, better than an elegant youth). This proverb, which appears in Act IV of *Celestina*, has passed down to modern times in the form of a rhyming couplet: *Con pan y vino/se anda el camino*— lit.: with bread and wine the route/way is walked. In other words if you want good results from your workers, they must be well fed; a similar notion is expressed in the English saying: An army marches on its stomach.

As mentioned earlier, the paroemiologist Sebastián de Horozco, in his collection entitled *Teatro universal de proverbios*, paraphrases some 3,145 proverbs in verse—all in *décima* form (stanzas of ten octosyllabic lines in full rhyme). Fray Luis de Escobar is another writer who, in his *Quinientos Proverbios de consejos y avisos en forma de letanía* (Five Hundred Proverbs of Advice and Warning in Litany Form), uses a proverb as the starting point for each of his five hundred verses; for example, *El abad de donde canta yanta*, meaning: For the abbot will eat where he sings for his meat. This proverb, teaching that each person should maintain himself through his own work, first appears in *Refranes que dicen las viejas* (278), and later in *Quijote* (II, 71). It is also glossed in prose by both Mal Lara, in his *Philosophia Vulgar* (Popular Philosophy), and Sebastián de Covarrubias, in his *Tesoro de la lengua castellana* (Treasury of the Spanish Language). However, Escobar and Horozco adopt the poetic form for their commentary on the proverb's origin, seen in the following *cantares*, given here along side a literal translation in English:

Del comer sin trabajar,	Of eating without working,
Pues que de allí se levanta:	This has given rise to:
El abad donde canta	Wherever the abbot sings
Ende tome el ayantar;	Here he is fed;
Libera nos, Domine.	Deliver us, Lord.
	(Fray Luis de Escobar)

Justo es que cada cual	It is just that he
trabajando sea pagado	Who works be paid
de su trabajo y jornal	For his work and time,
porque aqueste es su caudal	As this is his due
después de haber trabajado.	After having worked.
Y de aquesto se levanta	And this gives rise
aquel decir y proviene	To that maxim whose
	provenance is:
que el abad de donde canta	Wherever the abbot sings
de allí se dice que yanta	From this it is said he eats,
y se sustenta y mantiene.	Is nourished and maintained.
	(Sebastián Horozco)

Another example is the satirical proverb first recorded by Santillana: *Amor de monja y fuego de estopa y viento de culo, todo es uno* (A nun's love and fire of hemp and wind from the arse, it's all the same.) Again this is glossed in prose by both Vallés and Mal Lara, the latter explaining its meaning as: a thing that is flimsy is soon set alight, but its flames are soon extinguished. Sebastián de Horozco's *décima* gloss on this is as follows:

La monja que está metida	The nun that is locked
dentro de siete paredes,	Within seven walls,

¿qué aprovecha ser querida	What good does it serve to love her
pues no puede ser habida	If she cannot be had,
ni vista sino por redes?	Nor seen, except through grills?
Está siempre tras pavés	She is always shielded;
que aun tocárselo en su ropa	Even to touch her habit
no es posible ni podés	Is impossible and forbidden.
amor de monja en fin es	A nun's love is thus
como el fuego de la estopa.	Like a fire of hemp.

The same relationship that exists between proverbs and the oral tradition of popular lyric also exists between proverbs and the verse of the renowned 'cultured' poets of Spanish literature. However, as Alatorre remarks, it is not always possible to distinguish the boundaries between the popular and cultured veins. Correas, for example, uses a satirical poem written in a popular mode to gloss the proverb: *Niña, si quieres ventura, tómale clérigo, que dura,* which exalts the lasting nature of a priest's love, while at the same time criticizing the hypocrisy and sham sanctimoniousness of many ecclesiastics:

Niña, si quieres ventura,	Girl, if you want fortune,
tómale clérigo, que dura:	Take a priest, who'll endure:
el casado se va a su casa,	The married man goes home [at night],
y el que es soltero se casa,	And the bachelor will take a wife,
y el fraile también se muda;	And the friar also changes dwellings;
tómale clérigo, que dura.	Take a priest, who'll endure.

The above rhyme extolling the advantages of having a priest as a lover, and for which he is much in demand, also brings to mind the ironic ballad about a local priest, written by the seventeenth-century *culterano* poet Góngora. In the stanza below, ecclesiastical cant is lampooned by a play on the word *padre*, which in Spanish can mean both priest and father.

Comadres me visitaban,	My women friends would visit me,

que en el pueblo tenía	Of which in the town I
muchas;	had many;
ellas me llamaban padre,	They would call me father,
y taíta sus criaturas.	And their children dada.

The general belief in the unrivaled expertise as a lover of the priest or friar was engraved in maxims such as: *No le tomes menos, sino mozo y fraile* (Don't settle for anything less than a young friar). The popular beliefs and opinions mirrored in such proverbs were the inspiration for Góngora's satirical lyric which highlights the amatory prowess of Friar García—which far exceeded that of starched poets, vain youths, greedy canons and enamoured knights. Góngora, the great *culterano* poet of the Golden Age, wrote this in the form of a *letrilla* (poem set to music and written in stanzas of octosyllabic lines, in full rhyme, with an amusing *estribillo*, refrain or chorus), the refrain and two stanzas of which are given below:

A toda ley, madre mía,	True it is, mother mine,
lo demás es necedad,	The rest is foolishness,
regalos de Señoría	Gifts from a Noble
y obras de Paternidad.	And works of Fatherhood.
Aunque muy ajenos son,	Though inconsistent they be,
Señora, mis verdes años	Madam, my green years
de maduros desengaños	of mature disillusionment
y perfecta discreción,	And perfect good sense,
oíd la resolución	Listen to the solution
que me dio el tiempo,	That life has given me, after
después	
que me diste al Marqués,	You gave me to the Marquis,
y yo me di a fray García:	I gave myself to Friar Garcia:
a toda ley, madre mía,	True it is, mother mine,
lo demás es necedad,	The rest is foolishness,
regalos de Señoría	Gifts from a Noble
y obras de Paternidad.	And works of Fatherhood.
......	......
Sólo a esos doy mi amor	Only to these do I give my love
y mis contentos aplico,	And my happiness I seek,
madre, al uno porque	Mother, the first because he's
es rico,	rich,

y al otro porque es hechor.	And the other because he's a doer.
Llévame el fraile el humor,	The friar brings me contentment,
el marqués me lleva	And the marquis take me in
en coche;	his coach;
démosle al uno la noche	Let's give the night to one
y al otro démosle el día.	And the day to the other.
A toda ley, madre mía,	True it is, mother mine,
lo demás es necedad,	The rest is foolishness,
regalos de Señoría	Gifts from a Noble
y obras de Paternidad.	And works of Fatherhood.

Góngora's work contains many satirical *letrillas* that are rooted in popular sayings. The famous adage *Ande yo caliente, y ríase la gente*, which appears in *Quijote* (II, 50) and *Criticón* (II, 203), was also the source of Góngora's celebrated *letrilla* which glosses the adage as follows:

Ande yo caliente,	I'm alright Jack,
y ríase la gente.	So let people laugh.
Traten otros del gobierno	Let others deal with the government
del mundo y sus monarquías,	Of the world and its kingdoms,
mientras gobiernan mis días	While my days will be governed
mantequillas y pan tierno,	By butter-cakes and fresh bread,
y las mañanas de invierno	And on winter mornings
naranjada y aguardiente,	Orange juice and brandy,
y ríase la gente.	So let people laugh.
Coma en dorada vajilla	Let him eat off golden plates,
el príncipe mil cuidados	The prince with a thousand cares
como píldoras dorados;	Like gilded pills;
que yo en mi pobre mesilla	But I on my humble table
quiero más una morcilla	Want no more than sausage
que el asador reviente,	Burst open on the grill,
y ríase la gente.	So let people laugh.

Cuando cubra las montañas	When the mountains are covered
de blanca nive el enero,	White with snow in January,
tenga yo lleno el brasero	Let me have my hearth full
de bellotas y castañas,	Of acorns and chestnuts,
y quien las dulces patrañas	And one to tell me sweet tales
del Rey que rabió me cuente,	Of the enraged King of old,
y ríase la gente.	So let people laugh.
Busque muy en hora buena	Let him search at early hour
el mercader nuevos soles;	The merchant for new suns;
yo conchas y caracoles	I'll look for scallops and snails
entre la menuda arena,	Among the fine sand,
escuchando a Filomena	Listening to the nightingale
sobre el chopo de la fuente,	On the poplar at the spring,
y ríase la gente.	So let people laugh.
Pase a media noche el mar,	Let him swim the sea at midnight,
y arda en amorosa llama	And burn with amorous flame,
Leandro por ver su dama;	Leander, to see his Lady;
que yo más quiero pasar	All I want to swim through
del golfo de mi lagar	The gulf of my winepress
la blanca o roja corriente,	Is the white or red current,
y ríase la gente.	So let people laugh.
Pues Amor es tan cruel,	Since Love is so cruel,
que de Píramo y su amada	That for Pyramus and his beloved
hace tálamo una espada	The marriage bed was a sword,
do se junta ella y él,	Where she and he were joined,
sea mi Tisbe un pastel,	Let my Thisbe be a pastry,
y la espada sea mi diente,	And the sword be my tooth,
y ríase la gente.	So let people laugh.

Again Góngora is the author of the satirical *letrilla* with an amusing refrain which is still much used today as a proverbial phrase: *Cuando pitos, flautas; cuando flautas, pitos* (lit: When whistles, flutes: when flutes, whistles), meaning that things usually turn out to the contrary of what one wanted or imagined:

Da bienes Fortuna	Fortune sends gifts
que no están escritos:	Not according to the book:

cuando pitos, flautas,	When whistles, it's flutes,
cuando flautas, pitos.	When flutes; it's whistles.
¡Cuán diversas sendas	What diverse paths
se suelen seguir	Are usually followed
en el repartir	When distributing
honras y haciendas!	Honours and estates!
A una da encomiendas	To some she gives rewards
a otros sambenitos.	On others she puts the blame.
Cuando pitos, flautas,	When whistles, it's flutes,
cuando flautas, pitos.	When flutes, it's whistles.
A veces despoja	Sometimes she strips
de choza y apero	of cottage and tools
al mayor cabrero,	the chief goatherd,
y a quien se le antoja	And whenever she chooses
la cabra más coja	The lamest goat
pare dos cabritos.	Gives birth to two kids.
Cuando pitos, flautas,	When whistles, it's flutes,
cuando flautas, pitos.	When flutes, it's whistles.
Porque en una aldea	Because in a hamlet
un pobre mancebo	A poor youth
hurtó sólo un huevo,	Stole just one egg,
al sol bambolea,	He swings in the sun,
y otro se pasea	And another walks free
con cien mil delitos.	From a hundred thousand crimes.
Cuando pitos, flautas,	When whistles, it's flutes,
cuando flautas, pitos.	When flutes, it's whistles.

Two other idioms using the whistle and flute metaphor which are much used today are: *entre pitos y flautas* (with one thing and another); and *por pitos y flautas* (somehow or other).

The *conceptista* writer Quevedo is another seventeenth-century poet whose sardonic *letrillas* gave rise to proverbs. Perhaps the best known of these burlesque lyrics, whose title and refrain have become engraved in proverbial speech, is the *letrilla* entitled *Poderoso caballero es don Dinero* (A powerful lord is Mr. Money):

Madre, yo al oro me	Mother, before gold I bow
humillo;	my head;
él es mi amante y mi	He is my lover and my beloved,
amado,	
pues, de puro enamorado,	For, out of pure affection,
de contino anda amarillo,	He shines ever more yellow,
que pues, doblón o sencillo,	For a gold doubloon or less,
hace todo cuanto quiero,	He does all that I wish of him.
poderoso caballero	A powerful lord
es don Dinero.	Is Mr. Money.
......	......
Es tanta su majestad	His majesty is such
(aunque son sus duelos	(Though his sufferings are few),
hartos),	
que aun con estar hecho	That even though he's
cuartos,	quartered
no pierde su calidad;	His quality remains true,
pero pues da autoridad	For then he gives his authority
al gañán y al jornalero,	To the farmhand and the
	labourer,
poderoso caballero	A powerful lord
es don dinero.	Is Mr. Money.
Nunca vi damas ingratas	I've never seen ladies disdainful
a su gusto y afición,	Of his taste or inclination,
que a las caras de un	For the faces of a goldpiece
doblón	
hacen sus caras baratas;	They cheapen their own faces;
y pues las hace bravatas	And then become boastful
desde una bolsa de cuero,	From inside a leather purse,
poderoso caballero	A powerful lord
es don dinero.	Is Mr. Money.
Más vale en cualquier tierra	Worth more in any land
(¡mirad si es harto sagaz!)	(Look what wisdom!)
sus escudos en la paz	His standards in time of peace
que rodelas en la guerra.	Than shields in time of war.
Pues al natural destierra	For he turns natives into exiles
y hace propio al forastero,	And foreigners into nationals.
poderoso caballero	A powerful lord
es don dinero.	Is Mr. Money.

The same sort of relationship that exists between proverbs and *cantares* also exists between proverbs and *comedias*. During the Golden Age the word *comedia* was used to refer to al! full-length Spanish plays, whether of a comic or dramatic nature. In the plays of dramatists such as Lope de Vega, Ruiz de Alarcón, Rojas Zorrilla, and Calderón de la Barca, often the citing of just part of a proverb—either within the body of the play or as the title— was sufficient to evoke a tale, anecdote, or fable, etc. from Spanish folklore. There are patent examples of plays whose titles have their origin in a well-known adage, or which were so popular that their epigrammatic titles soon became proverbial dicta. There are also numerous examples of plays sprinkled with popular maxims. This is seen even in the works of an intellectual and philosophical dramatist like Calderón, whose plays were meant to be repre-sented in the court theatre, rather than in *corrales* (courtyards and public squares that served as municipal theatres), where Lope's plays were first seen. In an allegorical and philosophical work like Calderón's *La vida es sueño* (Life is a Dream), for example, which is full of *culterana* metaphor, there are clear allusions to popular idioms and proverbs. These allusions serve various purposes: they evoke well-known tales, are colourful linguistic ornaments and, above all in such an allegorical work, they help maintain a link with the popular strain. An obvious example of such a proverbial allusion is found at the start of Act III, v. 2220, where Clarín (the comic servant of Rosaura) says: *Si llaman santo al callar* ... Here Calderón clearly alludes to the proverb: *Al buen callar llaman Sancho* (Sage Silence is Sancho's name), which advises moderation and discretion in speech. This proverb appears in *Quijote* (II, 43), *Guzmán de Alfarache* (II, 42), and *Criticón* (III, 203). Another version of the adage is: *A buen callar llaman santo* (Silence is saintly)—used in *Corbacho* (220), and *Refranes que dicen las viejas* (2). The origin of this proverb is uncertain, however it is thought that Sancho was a common name much used as a synonym in colloquial speech for *santo* (saint), or *bueno* (good).

At other times, the proverbial allusion is not so explicit. This is the case when, in Act I, vv. 252–63 of the same play, Rosaura, in her first encounter with Segismundo, says:

Cuentan de un sabio, que un día	They tell of a sage, who one day
tan pobre y mísero estaba,	So poor and wretched was his lot,
que sólo se sustentaba	That he sustained himself only
de unas yerbas que comía.	On leaves that he collected.
'¿Habrá otro', entre sí decía,	'Could there be one', he reflected,
'más pobre y triste que yo?'	'Poorer and sadder than I?'
Y cuando el rostro volvió,	Then turning round,
halló la respuesta, viendo	The answer he found,
que iba otro sabio cogiendo	Seeing a poorer sage collecting
las hojas que él arrojó.	The leaves he was rejecting.

The above *décima* is a clear gloss of the proverb: *Lo que uno desecha, otro lo ruega* (What one person disdains, another begs for), reminiscent of the biblical reference to the crumbs from the rich man's table. Probably the most well-known example in Spanish literature of a story on this theme is Don Juan Manuel's *El Conde Lucanor*, Example X: *De lo que acontesció a un hombre que por pobreza e mengua de otra vianda comía atramuzes* (Of what happened to a man who through poverty and lack of food ate lupin seeds). However, there is no evidence to suggest that this was Calderón's source of inspiration.

We also find the case in *La vida es sueño* (Life is a Dream) where reference is made to the proverbial refrain from one of Góngora's *letrillas* (Act V, vv.1218-9): *Clarín que rompe el albor/no suena mejor.* In this scene the servant Clarín threatens old Clotaldo with blackmail by indicating that, like another *clarín* (a bugle), he will blare out everything he knows for all to hear. Góngora's lyric begins: *Cantando estaban sus rayos* (Your rays were singing), and the refrain runs:

¡Ay cómo gime, mas, ay cómo suena,	Oh how it groans, and oh how it sounds,
gime y suena	Groans and sounds
el remo a que nos condena	The rowing to which we are condemned
el niño Amor!	By young Cupid!
Clarín que rompe el albor	The bugle that sounds reveille
No suena mejor	Could not sound better.

There are other plays by Calderón that take their titles from a well-known proverb, which, at the same time, serve as succinct summaries and morals of the works. For example, *Casa con dos puertas mala es de guardar* (A house with two entrances is difficult guard). This proverb was recorded by Santillana some two centuries earlier, in his collection *Sayings used by Old Women . . .* (698). Other epigrammatic phrases which serve as titles for Calderón's plays are: *El mayor monstruo los celos* (Jealousy is the greatest monster); *A secreto agravio, secreta venganza* (For a secret offence, secret vengeance); *Dar tiempo al tiempo* (Give time time). And although these do not appear in the Spanish *refranero*, the compressed wisdom and pithy teaching or admonition of their precepts is such that they have all the hallmarks of perfect adages.

The prodigious playwright Lope de Vega used part of a popular adage as the title of his play *El perro del hortelano* (The Gardener's dog). This, as we saw earlier, originated as an ancient Aesopic fable, and the complete adage is: *El perro del hortelano, ni come las berzas ni las deja comer* (The gardener's dog neither eats cabbage nor lets others eat it). We shall look at this proverb in more detail when dealing with its appearance in Fernando de Rojas' *La Celestina*.

Yet another dramatist of the Golden Age, Ruiz de Alarcón, also chose to use popular adages as titles for his plays, for example: *No hay mal que por bien no venga* (Every cloud has a silver lining); *Quien mal anda, mal acaba* (He who strays from the straight and narrow, comes to a bad end), and *Las paredes oyen* (Walls have ears). This latter has passed into the English language mainly, it is thought, via the seventeenth-century Shelton translation of *Don Quijote*, where it was used in Book II, chapter 48. Here a sad and wounded Don Quijote is lying awake in his bedchamber in the castle, his head in bandages and looking a sorry sight, when Doña Rodríguez, lady-in-waiting to the duchess and a renowned gossip, enters. Along with other tittle-tattle, she proceeds to inform the knight of the "truth" about the seemingly charming duchess's bad humours, in which she has heard the duchess abounds. She begins by whispering:

Y aun mi señora la duquesa . . . Quiero callar; que se suele decir que las paredes tienen oídos.
And even my lady the Duchess . . . Shush! . . . for they say walls have ears.

The proverbial title of a play by Rojas Zorrilla: *Entre bobos anda el juego* (It takes one to know one) is an adage which is still much used today. It is also recorded in the text of *Criticón* (III, 181), where it is used ironically to signal that two characters are equally astute or skillful. In his play entitled *No hay amigo para amigo* Rojas employs another adage, the complete version of which again appears in *Don Quijote* (II, 12) as: *No hay amigo para amigo: las cañas se vuelven lanzas* (A friend cannot find a friend; reeds become lances). In Cervantes' work, the proverb's meaning is made clear by Sancho as he reflects on the great friendship between his mule and his master's horse, and he comments that this is "to the great shame of men who are so regardless of its [friendship's] laws! Hence the saying: a friend cannot find a friend; reeds become lances." The reeds and lances allusion refers to a game of Moorish origin in which various teams, mounted on horseback, throw reeds at one another while defending themselves with their shields. But as so often happens with games, aggression creeps in and "reeds become lances".

Such proverbial pearls of wisdom, or little gems as Erasmus referred to them, constitute an important and rich seam throughout Golden Age literature. They were certainly employed in many genres as linguistic ornaments, usually issuing from the mouths of rustics: reflecting the down-to-earth wisdom, memorable turns of phrase, picararesque wit and folklore of the common man and woman. However, there was also an important cross-current of influence between proverbs and literature of this period. As we have seen, adages played a vital role as initiators: the inspirational nucleus or moral around which stories, satirical poems and *comedias* were built; and in turn, there are many instances where these genres served both as originators of proverbial dicta and preservers of oral tradition, for without them much of this colourful language would probably not have survived.

VI

Literary Classics and Folk Wisdom

Proverbs, colloquial sayings and slang expressions have been used from the very beginning in Spanish literature, both in poetry and prose, as manifestations of popular culture and folklore. Even as early as the turn of the 13TH century we can see many examples of this popular material in the first novel of knight-errantry *El libro del Caballero Zifar* (The Book of the Knight Zifar), or in the early 14TH century poetic work by the Archpriest of Hita *El Libro de Buen Amor* (The Book of Good Love). And Rojas' famous tragicomedy *La Celestina,* written in 1499, stands out for its use of proverbs and colourful language, most of which issued from the mouths of its plebian characters: servants, rustics, and the old procuress Celestina herself. But it was during the Golden Age that proverbs reached their zenith in Spanish literature. Cervantes, in particular, would elevate the adage to its status as a linguistic treasure via his personification of rustic, down-to-earth wisdom, Sancho Panza, *padre de los proverbios* (father of proverbs) as his wife described him, and whose family were born with their bellies stuffed with proverbs. However, with the decadence of the Baroque and the refinement, "good taste" and verisimilitude of the Enlightenment the aforementioned linguistic gems began to lose their status and were no longer considered as precious stones but as *antiguallas*—unpolished, worthless rocks from the uncultured past. It would not be until the second half of the nineteenth century, when the interest in local customs and habits and the cult of the regional and popular elements of Spanish life was under-scored, that *refranes* would start to recapture their rightful status in the works of Fernán Caballero. This line would be carried on in the realist novels of authors such as Galdós, who would include many well-known proverbs in his works, and continued in recent times in the writings of Cela and Delibes.

In this section we shall look at the way these linguistic gems have been used in some of the most celebrated works of Spanish literature. It is in no way meant to be exhaustive, since that would would clearly be an immense task requiring several tomes. We have therefore focused here on just a few of the most pivotal works in which popular speech, proverbial dicta and folk wisdom have played an important role.

Written Testimony of Proverbs in Spanish Literature

El Libro del Caballero Zifar

As mentioned, one of the first books in Spanish literature in which folk wisdom plays a prominent role is *El libro del Caballero Zifar* (The Book of the Knight Zifar), written towards the end of the thirteenth century. This work is considered to be the first chivalristic novel in Spanish and relates the adventures of the protagonist and his son, whose exploits also serve a didactic purpose. In spite of the flights of fancy appropriate to works about knights-errant, the book is written in a down-to-earth, real-istic tone, in which the moral sobriety of the knight Zifar is of prime importance. The book contains numerous proverbs and expressions of folk wisdom which were in oral use in their time, many of which have endured down the ages, since versions of them are still in use today. Typical examples of these are:

Lo que ve el ojo, desea el corazón (Z.115)—What the eye sees, the heart desires. This proverbs was later recorded by Correas in his *Vocabulario de refranes*, but in its negative form: *Lo que los ojos no ven, el corazón no desea*—What the eye doesn't see, the heart doesn't grieve for/out of sight, out of mind, (272). Another variation is: *Ojos que no ven, corazón que no llora/siente*, which is recorded by Santillana (509) and later by Cervantes in *Quijote*

II, 67, as: *Ojos que no ven, corazón que no quiebra.* This saying, still much used today in Spanish, as well as in many other languages, can be traced to the beginning of the 12TH century, to St Bernard's fifth sermon, where he quotes it as a popular dictum used by the *vulgo*, common man, of his time: *Vulgo dicitur: Quod non videt oculus cor non dolet.*

A hombre de buen entendimento, pocas palabras cumplen (Z.428)—A word to the wise. In Santillana (78), and Mateo Alemán's picaresque novel *Guzmán de Alfarache* (IV, 125), it appears in the version which is commonly used today: *A buen entendedor, pocas palabras.* Cervantes also put these words into Sancho's mouth in *Quijote* (II, 37), where we hear the squire say to his master: *"Y en estas cosas, según he oído decir a vuesa merced, tanto se pierde por carta de más que por carta de menos; y al buen entendedor pocas palabras."* (And in such things, as I have heard your Worship say, one loses the game just the same with a card too many as a card too few; and a word to the wise is enough). The proverb must have been of such common currency at the end of the fifteenth century that when it appears in *Celestina* (Act VIII, 180) only the first part needed to be mentioned, when the servant Sempronio declares: *"Acuérdate, si fueres por conserva, apañas un bote para aquella gentencilla, que nos va más y a buen entendedor . . ."* (Remember, if you go looking for preserved fruit, get a jar for you know who, we could do with it, and a word to the wise . . .).

Quien a buen árbol se allega, buena sombra le cubre (Z.131)—He who stands under a good tree, will be well sheltered. This adage alludes to the advantages of seeking the company of those who have things that could be of use to us. Again, the proverb must have been in such common use that a century later when Rojas incorporates it in *Celestina* (Act VIII, 176) he only needs to mention a version of the first part: *Quien a buen árbol se arrima . . .* Cervantes uses both this and two other related proverbs in *Quijote* (II, 32), when Sancho confirms that he is indeed the person to whom his master has promised an island and that he well deserves such a prize:

Soy quien «júntate a los buenos y serás uno de ellos», y soy yo de aquellos «no con quien naces, sino con quien paces», y de los «quien a buen árbol se arrima buena sombra la cobija». Yo me he arrimado a buen señor, y ha muchos meses que ando en su compañía, y he de ser otro como él.

I am one of those who believe «keep the company of respectable people and you will be one of them,» and «not with whom you were bred, but with whom you have fed;» and «he who leans against a good tree, will find good shelter.» I have stuck close to my master for many months and will become such as he.

This proverb also appears in the first and last chapters of the picaresque novel *Lazarillo de Tormes*. In the first chapter the young *pícaro* Lazarillo, speaking about his mother's bad luck in life, says: "*Mi viuda madre, como sin marido y sin abrigo se viese, determinó arrimarse a los buenos . . .*" (As my widowed mother saw herself without husband and protector, she decided she would mix with people of value . . .).

No da Dios pan sino en ero sembrado (Z.119)—God doesn't give bread except from a sowed field. Two other proverbs with the same sentiments used in this work and which are equivalent to the English adage: God helps those who help themselves, are: *Ayúdate bien y ayudarte ha Dios* (Z.199), and *Quien se guarda, Dios le guarda* (Z.398). These proverbs underscore the voluntaristic element in the relationship between God and human kind. The modern version most used nowadays is: *A Dios rogando y con el mazo dando*—lit.: Pleading with God, but working with the mallet. However, on other occasions *Zifar* refers to the deterministic nature of man's relationship with the Divine. For example: *Aquel es guardado, el que Dios quiere guardar* (Z.189, 382 and 398)—God helps those he wants to help. In the seventeenth century Correas records this as: *Guardado es el que Dios guarda* (C.225).

Del decir al hacer mucho hay (Z.198)—lit: Between saying and doing there's a great distance. In modern times the proverb takes the form recorded in *Quijote* (II, 34 and 64): *Del dicho al hecho hay gran trecho*—Between the word and the deed there's a great stretch. This is often translated with a slightly different emphasis as: There's many a slip 'twixt cup and lip.

Quien bien see, no hay por qué se lieve (Z. 34 and 35)—A person who is happy/well situated where he is, does not move. The old Spanish word *see* means to remain or stay in a place or situation, while *lieve* means to leave or move. Don Juan Manuel (1282-1348) in his work *Conde Lucanor* (a didactic work infused with Medieval moralizing ideology, in which the Count Lucanor asks for advice from his servant Patronio) cites this proverb in chapter XXV as being a well known saying used by the old women of Castile: *Don Joan puso hi una palabra que dicen las viejas en Castilla, et la palabra dice así: quien bien se see, no se lieve* (Don Joan mentions here a saying used by old women in Castile, and the saying goes: a person who is well situated where he is, does not move.) Some five centuries later Fernán Caballero, in *Refranes y máximas populares recogidas en los pueblos del campo* (Proverbs and Maxims recorded in Country Villages) refers to the version that is most used today: *Quien bien está, no se mueva* (259).

El que no ha, no da (Z.306)—You can't give what you don't have. In *Celestina* (Act XVIII, 272) the proverb is put into the mouth of Centurio as: *Ninguno da lo que no tiene.* A more expressive form is recorded by Santillana (454) and later in seventeenth century by Gracián in his *Criticón* (III, 209): *Más da el duro que el desnudo*—The hard man gives more than the naked.

Other very familiar moralistic proverbs used in *Zifar* are:

Haz bien y no cates a quién. (Z. 343 and 353; also Santillana 331)—Do good and don't think for whom. The modern version of this is: *Haz bien y no mires a quién*—Do good and don't look at whom [you are doing it for]. (*Criticón*, III, 205).

Quien tal hace, tal prenda (Z.127)—You've made your bed, now lie on it. In *Guzmán de Alfarache* (II,147) this appears as: *Quien tal hace, que así lo pague*—As you act, so shall you pay [the consequences]; a variant of: As you sow, so shall you reap.

No es rico el que más ha, mas el que menos codicia (Z. 14 and 111)—He is not rich who has most, but who envies least.

Más vale saber que haber (Z.293; also Santillana 440)— Knowledge is worth more than possessions.

Más vale arte que ventura. (Z.360)—It's better to rely on skill than fortune.

El Libro de Buen Amor

Juan Ruiz, The Archpriest of Hita (1283–1350) is considered one of the greatest Spanish poets of the Middle Ages. He was the first poet to conjoin two contrasting linguistic strands: ordinary, every-day discourse including slang expressions used in the streets and market places, and poetic language of great lyricism. A large number of proverbs and idioms are incorporated into his poetic compositions, which help to create the impression of popular, realistic and down-to-earth speech. Such devices also give his poetry a very expressive edge as well as a lively tone. His most important and well-known work, *El Libro de Buen Amor* (The Book of Good Love), is one in which the interplay between lyrical and prosaic language, and ethereal and mundane sensations is used most effectively. It employs such proverbial sayings as:

Cuita no ha ley (v. 928)—Necessity knows no law. By 1528, the date of the publication of *Retrato de la Lozana andaluza* by Francisco Delicado, this proverb had been transcribed into more modern Spanish, and appeared as: *A la necesidad no hay ley*, which is very close to the modern version: *La necesidad carece de ley.* Another axiom on the theme of necessity cited in *El Libro de Buen Amor* (930) is: *Vieja con cuita trota*, or as it is known nowadays: *La necesidad hace a la vieja trotar*— Necessity makes the old woman trot. The theme of necessity will also appear very prominently in *Celestina* and *Lazarillo*, as we shall see later.

Engaña a quien te engaña, a quien te fai, faile (1466)— Deceive those who deceive you, and do unto others as they do unto you. This proverb, of French origin, also appears in the great collections of the Golden Age, such as those of Hernán Nuñez and Correas.

No hay mala palabra si no es a mal tenida (64)—Words are only bad if they are taken badly. The modern version is: *No hay palabra mal dicha si no fuese mal entendida*—a proverb that reprimands those who interpret maliciously what was said without malice.

No hay pecado sin pena ni bien sin galardón (933)—No sin goes unpunished, nor good unrewarded. This proverb clearly reflects the moralizing spirit of the Middle Ages, and is one that has remained unchanged up to the present time.

El can que mucho lame, sin duda sangre saca (616)—lit.: The dog that licks a lot, without doubt draws blood; meaning: too much affection is dangerous.

Quien mucho habla, yerra (733)—He who talks too much, errs exceedingly. A century later Santillana records this as: *Mucho hablar, mucho errar* (427), and his contemporary the Archpriest of Talavera in his work *Corbacho* writes: *Aquel que mucho habla, de necesario conviene de errar*—He who talks a lot, of necessity makes mistakes.

Más vale buen amigo que mal marido (1327)—Better a good friend [lover] than a bad husband. In *Celestina* (Act XVI, 261) this appears in the mouth of the young heroine, Melibea, when she says: "*No piensen en estas vanidades ni en estos casamientos; que más vale ser buena amiga que mala casada.*" (They need not bother about such trifling things as marriage, for it is better to be a good mistress than a bad wife).

PROVERBIOS MORALES

A contemporary of Arcipresete de Hita was the Rabbi don Sem Tob ben Ishaq Ardutiel—Santob de Carrión (c.1290-1369). His most important work was *Proverbios morales*—a book of moralizing, didactic poems, written in the form of quartets of heptasyllablic lines. Many of these proverbs have remained popular to this day. Examples of these are:

Cierto es y no fallece	True it is and without fail
proverbio todavía:	This proverb yet:
el huésped y el pece	That guests and fish
hieden al tercero día	Stink after three days.

Here the expression *no fallece* means *no falla* (without fail), thus the author, in the first two lines, underscores what was mentioned earlier regarding the value placed on proverbs as enshrining some universal truth. The proverb: Guests and fish stink after three days, was first recorded by the Roman playwright Plautus (c.254–184 BC) in his work *Miles Gloriousus*, and has struck such a resonant chord down the ages that versions of it are found in many languages still.

Other examples of Sem Tob's proverbial quartets are:

Del hombre vivo dicen	Of the living,
las gentes sus maldades,	People besmirch their name,
desque muerto bendicen	Once dead,
cuento de sus bondades.	Their goodness they acclaim.

Si fuese el hablar	If talking were
de plata figurado,	Of a silver mould,
debe ser el callar	Silence would be
de oro afinado.	Of polished gold.

Porque todo hombre vea	So that every man should see
que en el mundo cosa	That in this world things
no hay del todo fea	Neither all ugly
ni del todo hermosa.	Nor all beautiful be.

No hay cosa más larga	There is nothing so long
que lengua de mentiroso,	As a liar's tongue,
ni hay fin más amarga	Nor end more bitter
de comienzo sabroso.	Than a sweet beginning.

El Corbacho

Alfonso Martínez de Toledo, otherwise referred to as the Archpriest of Talavera (1398–c.1470), is best known for his didactic work *El Corbacho*, in which *el habla popular*—idioms, slang expressions and proverbial phrases—takes on aesthetic value in the author's prose. *El Corbacho* is full of popular idioms recorded directly from the mouths of ordinary people in the streets and market places. The work sermonizes in particular on the evils of courtly love, which the Archpriest regards as lust. It is a deeply misogynistic work that takes every opportunity to castigate what the author sees as the venality and degeneracy of deceitful and wicked women. It uses all the natural resources of colloquial language: numerous exclamations, reiterations, rhetorical questions, as well as proverbs as a concise means of encapsulating the folkfore of the time. This results in a prose style that is at once dynamic, colourful and expressive. It also incorporates verbal insults commonly heard in street life coming from the mouths of women. Such is the case when the Archpriest berates marriages between old men and young girls. First the girl curses her parents for giving her into such a union as she gets into bed with her old husband. She then curses the old man himself with a prayer that runs: *¡Mala postrimería, malos días, malos años le dé Dios, amén!*—May God give him a bad end, bad days, bad years, amen! (226). This continues with a monologue by the girl, once she has blown out the candle and turned her back on the old man, saying:

> *¡Mala vejez, mala postrimería te dé Dios, viejo podrido, maldito de Dios y de sus santos, corcobado y perezoso, sucio y gargajoso, bellaco y enojoso, pesado más que de plomo, áspero como cazón, duro como buey, tripudo como ansarón, cano, calvo y desdentado! ¿Y aquí te echaste cabe mí, diablo desazado, huerco espantadizo, puerco invernizo, en el verano sudar y en el invierno temblar?* (226-7)

May God give you a bad old age, a bad end, rotten old man, damned by God and his saints, hunchbacked and lazy, dirty and spitting, vile and crotchety, heavier than lead, coarse as dog fish, hard as an ox, paunchy as a goose, grey, bald and toothless! And you lie by my side, insipid devil, scary hell, wintry pig, you sweat in the summer and shiver in the winter?

The book is full of blaspheming or swearing on one's own life:

> *¡Qué noramala nací! ¡Mal punto vine aquí! ¡Dolores que vos maten, rabia que vos acabe, diablo, huerco, maldito!* (226)

Curse the day I was born! I came into this world at a bad time! May pain kill you, may rabies finish you off, you devil, hell, accursed one!

¡Nunca goce de mi alma! ¡El diablo me lleve! ¡El diable me ahogue! ¡El diablo sea señor de mi alma! (171)
I never enjoyed my soul! The devil take me! The devil choke me! The devil be the Lord of my soul!

In addition to the above-mentioned colourful idioms, the book brims with proverbs such as:

Cuando la barba de tu vecino vieres pelar, pon la tuya en remojo (104)—When you see your neighbour's beard being shaved off, put yours in soak; meaning: at the first sign of danger, get prepared, lest the same thing should happen to you. The version used nowadays is the one recorded in *El Criticón* (III, 207) as: *Cuando la barba de tu vecino veas pelar, echa la tuya a remojar*. In former times is was considered a great offence to cut off a man's beard, and the proverb warns that one should learn from other people's mistakes.

Más sabe el loco en su casa que el cuerdo en la ajena (116)—The madman knows more in his own house than the sane man in another's. Gracian, in *El Criticón* (III, 202) changes this to: *Más sabe el necio en su casa que el sabio en la ajena*—The fool knows more in his own house than the wise man in another's. In *Quijote* (II, 43) Sancho Panza uses the proverb to his master after reciting a litany of adages, to which Don Quijote replies, refuting his squire's pearls of rustic wisdom, that the fool knows nothing either in his own house or in anyone else's.

Mal de muchos, gozo es (122)—The misfortune of many is a joy. In *El Criticón* (III, 204) this appears in two similar forms but with opposite meanings: *Mal de muchos, consuelo de todos*—Misfortune of many, consolation of all; and: *Mal de muchos, consuelo de tontos*—Misfortune of many, consolation of fools; this latter being the guise it usually takes today.

Uno dice por la boca, otro tiene al corazón (171)—What she says is one thing, what she believes is another. This proverb appears at the beginning of chapter six in the misogynistic context of the Archpriest sermonizing on how women are hypocrites and have two faces: "*La mujer ser de dos faces y cuchillo de dos tajos no hay duda en ello, por cuanto de cada día vemos que uno dice por la boca, otro tiene al corazón.*" (Women have two faces and are a knife of two edges [double-edged sword] there is no doubt of that, from what we can see every day what she says is one thing, what she believes is another). This proverbial image of woman as a hypocrite is a Biblical one that was promulgated for example in *Proverbs* 5,3-4, where it says: "For the lips of a strange woman drop as honeycomb/And her mouth is smoother than oil/But her end is bitter as wormwood,/Sharp as a two edged sword."

Según dice el antiguo proverbio: "Mientras que rico fueres, ¡oh, cuántos puedes contar de amigos!; empero si los tiempos se mudan y anublan, ¡ay, que tan solo te hallaras!" (72)—As the old proverb says: When rich, how many you can count as friends! But if times change and storm clouds gather, Ah, how lonely you will be! This refers to a maxim taken from Ovid's *Tristia*: *Donec eris felix, multos numerabis amicos: tempora si fuerint nubila, solus eris.*

Por tanto se dice: "Guarda qué dices, que las paredes a las horas oyen y orejas tienen." (293)—It is therefore said: Watch what you say, for walls hear and have ears.

El ajo y el vino atriaca es de los villanos (97)—Garlic and wine is the peasant's remedy. This refers to the belief of the time that garlic and wine had curative properties and were the best remedy for most illnesses and a good antidote for stings and wounds.

LA CELESTINA

In 1499, a year before the the publication of the *Adages* of Erasmus, the tragi-comedy of Calisto and Melibea, *La Celestina*, appeared in Spain. In this work Fernando de Rojas (c.1457-1541) brings together medieval and Renaissance elements. The medieval element is underscored by the work's moralising purpose, which was the censure of passionate love. The Renaissance element is highlighted by the pagan environment in which enjoyment of life is the motivating principle, and the complete disregard for any Christian teaching on the part of the characters. The cultured strain in the work is noted particularly in the insipient human-istic tendency to use elegant discourse and Latinized terms, all of which appear mainly in the speech of the well-bred lovers Cal-isto and Melibea. However the cultured speech and erudite allu-sions of Calisto and Melibea are found along side the vivid and down-to-earth language of the servant class, whose speech reflects a wealth of idioms and proverbial wisdom, in the manner of *El Corbacho*. Rojas' skill in combining the popular and cultured strains in this work led Juan de Valdés in his *Diálogo de la lengua* (178) to proclaim that "*ningún libro hay escrito en castellano donde la lengua está más natural, más propria ni más ele-gante.*" (there is no other book written in Spanish where the language is more natural, more apt and more elegant). In this study, it is the popular aspect of the Spanish language that most interests us.

Rojas inserts a veritable anthology of adages in the mouths of his characters, particularly those of the disloyal servants, Sem-pronio and Pármeno, and above all in the mouth of the astute witch and procuress, Celestina. The beauty of Rojas' use of proverbs in this way is that they are used aptly in realistic contexts which gives the work a vital and energetic style, full of expressive language. In *Celestina*, straightforward proverbs appear along side allusions to adages which are turned into idiomatic or slang expressions. Such devices are used ingeniously to bring the lan-guage alive. Proverbial dicta fall naturally from characters' lips without any artifice or contrivance. They flow as spontaneous utterances of the plebian tongue which express the thoughts and feelings of ordinary people. In this work Rojas follows in the foot-steps of the Archpriest of Talavera in his work *El Corbacho*, where popular speech achieves a natural beauty in its own right, and where the language—intoned in adages, proverbial phrases, collo-quialisms and slang—is stamped by lively chat, dynamism and colour.

One of the most noticeable aspects of *Celestina* is the extent to which proverbs are known and recited; so much so that occa-sionally the characters don't even feel the need to finish them. They are left suspended halfway through, sometimes followed by an *etcétera*, or ellipses, or just alluded to by making the merest suggestion to a few words from a well-known adage.

In many forceful passages such torrents of proverbial speech take the form of adages in their original and complete form, together with variations and adaptations. Such is the case when Celestina, in Act VII, advises the young prostitute Aréusa to take two lovers, just as her cousin has done. The Procuress then recites a litany of popular proverbs (discussed individually in the English translation below) to prove her point that one of anything is not enough, and alone one can do nothing:

> *Una alma sola ni canta ni llora; un solo acto no hace hábito; un fraile solo pocas veces lo encontrarás por la calle; una perdiz sola por maravilla vuela, mayormente en verano; un manjar solo continuo presto pone hastío; una golondrina no hace verano; un testigo solo no es entera fe; quien sola una ropa tiene, presto la envejece . . .*

Looking at the meaning, as well as the use various other writers have made of some of the aphorisms recited by Celestina above, we find that:

> The first phrase, *Una alma sola ni canta ni llora*—A single soul neither sings nor weeps, is a well-known proverb that was also recorded by Santillana (703). But a century before, the Archpriest of Hita, in his *Libro de Buen Amor* (111), cites a different version: *Una ave sola, ni bien canta ni bien llora* (A single bird neither sings nor crys well).

> *Un solo acto no hace hábito*—A single act does not make a habit. This is recorded later by Correas (496) in his collection of proverbs.

> *Un fraile solo pocas veces lo encontrarás por la calle*—You will rarely find a friar walking alone in the street.

> *Una perdiz sola por maravilla vuela, mayormente en verano*—It would be a great surprise to see a single partridge fly, especially in the summer. This axiom from rural life refers to the fact that the partridge is essentially a terrestrial and sociable bird, that does not often take to the sky.

Un manjar solo continuo presto pone hastío—A single delicacy eaten continually soon repels. Also recorded in Correas (495).

Una golondrina no hace verano—One swallow doesn't make a summer. This proverb really constitutes the nucleus of the passage, not only in its physical position in the centre of the speech, but also for its verbal formula rooted in the classics. The other inductive maxims revolve around this central core to reinforce its popular wisdom with an accumulation of different images taken from observation of life. The proverb was recorded in the *Adages* of Erasmus (I, vii) in its Latin form: *Una hirundo no facit ver*. In Spain it appeared in writing at least half a century earlier in Santillana's *Refranes que dicen las viejas* (704); also later in *Quijote* (I, 13). Nowadays it is more commonly heard in Spanish as: *Ni un dedo hace mano, ni una golondrina verano*—One finger doesn't make a hand, nor one swallow a summer.

Un testigo solo no es entera fe—One witness alone is not sufficiently reliable.

Quien sola una ropa tiene, presto la envejece—He who has only one set of clothes, soon wears them out.

All these variations on a theme are used by Celestina to convince the young girl that one lover is not enough. She concludes by advising her to "Take at least two [lovers], its recommendable. You have two ears, two feet, two hands, two sheets on your bed, two chemises to change!"—a clear example of the work's encouragement of the enjoyment of life and its flouting of Christian moral teaching and asceticism, for which it was much criticized, even by Cervantes.

It often seems impossible for Celestina to cite a single proverb to prove her point, a second or third adage has to be brought in to drive the message home. An example of this is found in Act IV, at Celestina's first meeting with the young noble woman, Melibea, who asks the procuress if she yearns to be young again. To this Celestina replies that she does not, for:

Tan presto, señora, se va el cordero como el carnero. Ninguno es tan viejo, que no puede vivir un año, ni tan mozo, que hoy no pudiese morir. Así que en esto poca ventaja nos lleváis.

It is just as easy, madam, for the lamb to go [to the slaughter] as the sheep. No-one is so old that he cannot live another year, nor so young that he could not die today. So that in this you have little advantage over me.

The first phrase is an adage that later appears in *Don Quijote* (II, 7), where Sancho tells his master:

> ...*que como vuesa merced mejor sabe, todos estamos sujetos a la muerte, y que hoy somos y mañana no, y que tan presto se va el cordero como el carnero, y que nadie puede prometerse en este mundo más horas de vida de las que Dios quisiere darle*...

> ...that, as your worship knows, we are all subject to death: here today and gone tomorrow; and that the lamb goes [to the slaughter] as soon as the sheep, and that nobody can promise himself a longer life than God wishes to grant him ...

A modern variant of this is: *A la losa tan presto va la vieja como la moza* (The old woman and the young girl go just as easily to the grave).

Both in *Celestina* and *Quijote* this proverb is inserted naturally and unobtrusively into the dialogue. In order to achieve this harmonious effect in a character's speech, adages sometimes undergo a spontaneous transformation, as is the case with this particular proverb when it again appears in *Quijote* a few chapters later, (II, 20):

> *A buena fe, señor -respondió Sancho-, que no hay que fiar en la descarnada, digo, en la muerte, la cual también come cordero como carnero; y a nuestro cura he oído decir que con igual pie pisaba las altas torres de los reyes como las humildes chozas de los pobres.*

> "Truly, Sir," replied Sancho, "there is no trusting the skeleton, that is, Death, which devours the lamb as easily as the sheep; and I have heard our priest say it tramples equally on the high towers of kings and on the humble cottages of the poor."

This last phrase is taken from Horace: *Pallida mors aequo pulsat pede pauperrum tabernas requmque turres*, and since it was not fitting for a rustic like Sancho to quote such an erudite dictum, it was credited to the priest.

In Act XII the servants Sempronio and Parmeno go to Celestina's house to demand from the old bawd their share in the reward for arranging the union between the young lovers Calisto and Melibea. When the procuress refuses to hand this over, Sempronio comments:

No es la primera vez que yo he dicho cuánto en los viejos reina este vicio de la codicia. «Cuando pobre, franca; cuando rica, avarienta.» Así que adquiriendo crece la codica, y la pobreza codiciando, y ninguna cosa hace pobre al avariento sino la riqueza. ¡Oh Dios, y cómo crece la necesidad con la abundancia! ¡Quién la oyó esta vieja decir que me llevase yo todo el provecho, si quisiese, de este negocio, pensando que sería poco! Agora que lo ve crecido, no quiere dar nada, por cumplir el refrán de los niños que dicen: «De lo poco, poco; de lo mucho, nada.»

This is not the first time I have said that avarice is the worst fault of old people! «If poor, open-handed, if rich, tight-fisted!» So avarice increases with possessions, and poverty with covetousness. And nothing makes the miser so poor as wealth! O God, and how needs increase with abundance! This old woman told me to take all the profit from this affair if I wanted to, thinking it would be little. Now, seeing how much there is she wants to give nothing away. Thus she confirms the old saying: «From little, little; from much, nothing.»

The last proverb cautions: the more people have, the more they want, and serves to reinforce that the rich are tight-fisted.

In addition to the above examples in which Rojas employs clusters of proverbs, *La Celestina* is also liberally sprinkled with single adages used as concise and colourful linguistic devices to express a particular idea. For example, in the same scene as above (Act XII), Sempronio tells Celestina that his master has already been very generous to him and he could not be so greedy as to ask for more. He advocates restraint with this proverb:

Contentémonos con lo razonable, no lo perdamos todo por querer que: «quien mucho abarca, poco suele apretar.»

Let us be content with a reasonable amount, and not lose all for «he who grasps all, loses all.» Nowadays the proverb is used to mean «don't take on too much».

Again, in Act VI, Pármeno makes sarcastic remarks about Celestina, who is talking to the young noble Calisto about Melibea. Pármeno turns aside and berating the old bawd's greed he starts his tirade: "*Tú dirás lo tuyo: «entre col y col, lechuga.»*" (As usual you will say: «between two cabbages, a lettuce»). This alludes to the old custom of sowing a lettuce between each pair of cabbages. The proverb is used to indicate a rest period between jobs, and at other times that a little variety enhances things generally.

Rojas is a master at adapting adages to specific contexts. For example in Act VII he alludes to a well-known adage by converting the first part into an idiom which he knows will be clearly understood by everyone, and which at the same time paints a succinct and apt description of the situation and character who is likened to the dog in a manger. The author then reinforces this by applying the adage's meaning directly to the case Celestina is arguing. Here Celestina tells the young prostitute Aréusa that it is a sin to make men sick with desire when a woman can so easily cure their sickness, and urges: "*No seas el perro del hortelano y pues tú no puedes de ti propia gozar, goce quien puede ...*" (Don't be like the dog in the manger, and as you can't enjoy it yourself, keep out those that can). As we saw earlier, this proverbial phrase *el perro del hortelano* alludes to a well-known adage recorded by Santillana in *Refranes que dicen las viejas*, where it appears as: *El perro del hortelano, ni come las berzas ni las deja comer* (lit: The gardener's dog neither eats cabbage nor lets others eat it). Today the proverb usually takes the form: *El perro del hortelano ni quiere las manzanas/berzas para sí ni para su amo* (lit: The gardener's dog neither wants apples/cabbage for himself nor wants his master to have them).

Later, in 1618, Lope de Vega would write a comedy entitled *El perro del hortelano*, which was inspired by this proverb, and which is referred to in the following lines from Act II of the play (vv.2297-99):

Es del hortelano el perro	It is the gardener's dog
ni come ni comer deja	Who neither eats nor lets others eat
ni está fuera ni está dentro	He is neither in nor out

And in Act III (vv.3070-71):

Diana ha venido a ser	Diana has become
el perro del hortelano	The dog in the manger.

Act XVI: Pleberio, the wealthy father of the heroine Melibea, when talking to his wife about the short and uncertain nature of life, says:"... *Y pues somos inciertos cuándo habemos de ser llamados, viendo tan ciertas señales, debemos echar nuestras barbas en remojo y aparejar nuestros fardeles ..."* (lit:...And as we are unsure when it may be our turn, seeing such obvious signs, we should put our beards in soak and prepare our bags ...).

As we saw in *Corbacho,* the proverb alluded to here is: *Cuando la barba de tu vecino vieras pelar, echa la tuya a remojar* (When you see your neighbour shave off his beard, put yours in soak; meaning: at the first signs of danger, get prepared). Once more, Rojas uses just part of the famous adage as a proverbial phrase in the sure knowledge that his readers will be very familiar with the allusion.

Act XVIII: The young prostitutes Elicia and Areúsa go to the house of the ruffian Centurio. Centurio tells them that he is poor and has few possessions, and illustrates this by saying:"*Las alhajas que tengo es el ajuar de la frontera: un jarro desbocado, un asador sin punta ..."* (lit: The jewels that I have are the goods from my household on the frontier: a cracked jug, a blunt roasting spit ...).The actual proverb is: *Ajuar de la frontera: dos estacas y una estera*—Goods from my household on the frontier: two pickets and a rush mat.

This adage makes reference to custom of the time, when soldiers who were garrisoned in villages on the frontier [between Christians and Moors] usually carried little baggage with them. In this case, Rojas' character is saying that like a soldier he has few belongings.

The above are just a few of the references that Rojas makes to well-known proverbs, most of which are taken from the anecdotes and stories told by old women sitting round the fire during the winter months. The work itself makes reference to this in the Prologue, echoing the title of Santillana's collection *Refranes que dicen las viejas tras el fuego*, it reads: "*Y si no pareciese conseja de tras el fuego . . .*" (And if it didn't give the impression of being a fireside tale . . .) Celestina constantly digs into her treasury of proverbs which she spouts to her circle of women friends, and which are accepted by them as irrefutable truths whose wisdom has stood the test of time. Pármeno in Act II discharges these whether or not they offend, with the result that, as he says: "*Mal me quieren mis comadres, etc.*" (The women in the village don't like me, etc.). This was recorded in Santillana (413) as: *Mal me quieren mis comadres porque digo las verdades*—The women in the village don't like me because I tell them the truth. These sentiments are again referred to in Act XV when Elicia tells her friend Areúsa "*que, como dicen: «riñen las comadres», etcétera.*" (as they say, quarreling women, etc.) The complete proverb is: *Riñen las comadres, y dícense las verdades*—Quarreling women disclose the truth (The angry tongue keeps no counsel).

In Act I, the servant Sempronio, when citing the well-known adage: *La mujer y el vino sacan al hombre de tino* (Women and wine drive men out of their mind) deliberates, evoking historians and philosophers and even Solomon:

> *Lee los historiales, estudia los filósofos, mira los poetas. Llenos están los libros de sus viles y malos ejemplos y de las caídas que llevaron los que en algo, como tú [Calisto], las reputaron. Oye a Salomón do dice que las mujeres y el vino hacen a los hombres renegar. Conséjate con Séneca y verás en qué las tiene. Escucha al Aristóteles, mira a Bernardo. Gentiles, judíos, cristianos y moros, todos en su concordia están.*

Read your historians, study the philosophers, look to the poets. Books are full of vile and wicked examples, and of the down-fall of those who, like you [Calisto], held women in high esteem. Listen to Solomon when he says that women and wine bring men to ruin. Consult Seneca and you will see how poorly he regards them. Listen to Aristotle, pay heed to Bernard. Gentiles, Jews, Christians and Moors, all are in agreement on this.

The lowly Sempronio may be speaking in this high-flown manner in order to please his master, the schooled and noble Calisto, and to persuade him to enlist the help of the old bawd Celestina. It was probably thought more appropriate here to invoke the wisdom of illustrious names of antiquity rather than the folk wisdom of common people.

Rather strangely and somewhat inappropriately, Celestina, in Act I, also resorts to citing the philosopher Seneca when she meets another of Calisto's servants, Parmeno, recalling how long it has been since she last saw him:

Sin duda, dolor he sentido, porque has por tantas partes vagado y peregrinado, que ni has provecho ni ganado deudo ni amistad. Que, como Séneca dice, los peregrinos tienen muchas posadas y pocas amistades, porque en breve tiempo con ninguno no pueden formar amistad.

Without doubt, I have felt sorrow, for you have wandered far and wide, and thus been unable to enjoy or win friendship. For as Seneca said, pilgrims have many resting places but few friends, since in such short stays they have no time to form real friendships with anybody.

Proverbs also lend a comic and lively tone to the expression of certain characters. For example, in Act IX Areúa, describing the wretched life that awaits a girl who serves a mistress, declares:

Así que esperan galardón, sacan baldón; esperan salir casadas, salen menguadas; esperan vestidos y joyas de boda, salen desnudas y denostadas. Estos son sus premios, éstos son sus beneficios y pagos. Oblíganse a darles maridos, quítanles el vestido.

Instead of presents they get insults; instead of marriage they end up in ignominy; instead of a dowry and wedding gifts they are turned out naked and disgraced. That's all her reward, her profit, her pay. She is promised a husband, and instead her very clothes are stripped from her.

Lazarillo de Tormes (anonymous 1554) was the first picaresque Spanish novel. Written in the form of autobiographical narrative, the work recounts in lively, spontaneous language, brimming with graphic realism, how a young boy from the lowest level of society wheedles and tricks his way upwards until, as an adult, he manages to survive and eventually achieve security as a lowly town crier in Toledo. *Lazarillo* does not display an anthology of proverbial dicta, nor does it revel in the slang expressions of the underworld seen in Cervantes' novel *Rinconete y Cortadillo*. However, in the opening chapter, when referring to his first master, the young Lazarillo says: "*Comenzamos nuestro camino, y en muy pocos días me mostró jerigonza.*" (We started our journey, and within a few days he taught me slang/jargon [the argot of vagabonds and tramps]. Yet this argot is not actually used in the text of the novel. Rather a balance is maintained between the sobriety of the cultured strain in the Spanish language and the colloquial, where *lo vulgar*, popular speech, comes to the fore. There are few proverbial maxims expressed in adages as such. Most are allusions to, or echoes of, proverbs or colloquial expressions in circulation at the time, which are converted into proverbial phrases that help the protagonist's narration of his life. Examples of such devices are:

Chapter 1, p.22: When Lazarillo has the opportunity to trick his first master, the astute but mean blind man, by substituting a rotten turnip for his juicy sausage, the young picaro says: "*Púsome el demonio el aparejo delante de los ojos, el cual, como suelen decir, hace al ladrón …*" (The devil put the means [temptation] in front of my eyes, which, as they say, makes the thief . . .)

Here he is clearly indicating a well-known proverb with the words, *como suelen decir,* (as they say), and making apt use of the adage: *El aparejo hace el ladrón*—The means makes a thief. This was also recorded a little later, in 1587, by Sánchez de Ballesta, along with another adage of similar meaning: *En arca abierta el justo peca*—Faced with an open trunk the pious would sin. The version most often heard nowadays is: *La ocasión hace al ladrón*—Opportunity makes a thief.

Chapter 1, p.10: Lazarillo refers to his impoverished mother's determination to: " ... *arrimarse a los buenos.*" This alludes to the proverb reviewed earlier in the section dealing with *El Libro del Caballero Zifar*, which runs: *Allégate a los buenos, y serás uno de ellos*—Stick close to good/useful people and you will become one of them. And in the last chapter, Lazarillo declares that this has been his guiding principle in life: " ... *yo determiné arrimarme a los buenos*" (I decided to stick close to useful people).

Chapter 2, p.36: While kept on starvation rations by his second master, the priest, Lazarillo reflects: " ... *pues dicen que el ingenio con ella [el hambre] se avisa, y al contrario con la hartura, y así era por cierto en mí*" (... they say that it [hunger] sharpens the wits, and the contrary with satiety, and that was certainly the case with me ...). Once again, the words *dicen que* (they say) is used to introduce a reference to a well-known proverb in circulation at the time. In Correas' collection this adage appears as: *La hambre despierta el ingenio* (hunger sharpens the wits).

In the same scene Lazarillo also declares: "*Como la necesidad sea tan grande maestra, viéndome con tanta siempre, ...* " (As necessity is such a great teacher, being in such a permanent state myself ...). This proverb was recorded by Erasmus in the *Adages* as *Necessitas magistra* (necessity is the mother of invention), and Correas cites it in his collection as: *La necesidad hace maestros.*

In la Celestina Act IX, Rojas puts the saying into Pármeno's mouth when he says: "*La necesidad y pobreza, la hambre ... no hay mejor maestra en el mundo, no hay mejor despertadora y avivadora de ingenios.*" (Necessity and poverty, hunger ... there is no better teacher in the world, there's no better awakener and sharpener of inventiveness). Nowadays the proverb runs: *La necesidad aguza el ingenio.*

Chapter 3, p.49: Referring to the dissembling contented demeanour of his proud, but impecunious and hungry, third master—the *escudero* (squire/gentleman)—a man who has hardly eaten a thing in days, Lazarillo exclaims: "*¡Bendito seáis Vos, Señor -quedé yo diciendo-, que dais la enfermedad y* *ponéis el remedio."* (Blessed art thou, Lord—I stood saying—for you send the illness but also send the remedy).

A few years later, this proverbial phrase was recorded by Sebastián de Horozco in his collection *Teatro universal de proverbios*, and also in *Quijote* (II, 19) as: *Dios cuando da la llaga, luego da la medicina* (God, when he gives the wound, then gives the medicine).

Chapter 3, p.53: Lazarillo, willing to share the little food he had with his unfortunate and penniless master, says: *"Con todo, parescióme ayudarle, pues se ayudaba y me abría camino para ello . . . "* (Still, I thought I should help him, for he was helping himself and showing me the way also . . .). Here there is a clear allusion to a common dictum of the time which, according to Sebastián de Covarrubias Horozco, seventeenth-century author of *Tesoro de la lengua castellana* (Treasury of the Spanish Language), advises: *Ayúdate y ayudarte he*—Help yourself and I will also help you.

In the same scene, the impoverished *escudero*, gentleman/ squire—after partaking of a meal of cow's foot, provided by his servant—says to Lazarillo: *"Dígote que es el mejor bocado del mundo y que no hay faisán que ansi me sepa"* (I tell you that it is the best meal there is, and no pheasant could taste better). This phrase adverts to the adage: *Más quiero en mi casa pan que en ajena faisán*—Better to eat bread in one's own home than pheasant in a neighbour's. It brings to mind another popular saying, again recorded by Sebastián de Horozco in his *Teatro universal de proverbios: Más vale pan con amor, que gallina con dolor*—Better eat dry bread with love, than chicken in sorrow.

Chapter 3, p.51: Lazarillo's master praises him for throwing himself on the mercy of the townsfolk and asking for food: *"Mas tú haces como hombre de bien en eso, que más vale pedillo [pedirlo] por Dios que no hurtallo [hurtarlo]"*, (But, you've behaved very decently here, for after all, it's better to beg in the name of God than to steal). This clearly alluded to the proverb: *Más vale pedir que hurtar*—It better to beg than steal.

There are many other clear insinuations to well-known proverbs in *Lazarillo*, for example:

Chapter 1, p.13: Here the blind man teaches the picaro his first lesson. He tells the boy to put his ear against a stone bull so that he can hear a loud noise inside. When Lazarillo complies, his master gives him a vicious blow, crashing his head against the statue and counsels: *"Necio, aprende, que el mozo del ciego, un punto ha de saber más que el diablo"* (Idiot, learn that a blind man's boy must know one trick more than the devil himself).

This expression is also found in *Quijote* (II, 23) as: *"Merlín, aquel francés encantador que dicen que fue hijo del diablo; y lo que yo creo es que no fue hijo del diablo, sino que supo, como dicen, un punto más que el diablo."* (Merlin that French wizard, whom they say was the devil's son; and I think he was not the devil's son, but knew, as they say, one trick more than the devil himself).

Prologue, p.5: Lazarillo muses on the fact that some benefit can be taken from most things, including the story of his life, and that in any case tastes vary: *" ... mas lo que uno no come, otro se pierde por ello. Y así vemos cosas tenidas en poco de algunos, que de otros no lo son."* (... what one man will not eat, another will die for. And so we see that things can be worthless for some, and not for others/ One man's meat is another man's poison).

Sebastián de Horozco in *Teatro universal de proverbios*, mentions two similar proverbs on a related theme: *Lo que uno desecha, a otro aprovecha* and *Lo que uno no quiere, otro lo ruega*, whose concept is equivalent to the crumbs from the rich man's table. The present-day version of these proverbs is made up of a combination of both: *Lo que uno desecha, otro lo ruega*—What one man discards, another begs for.

As mentioned, *Lazarillo* is also sprinkled with colourful idioms and slang expressions of the time. Examples of these are:

Yo vine aquí con este echacuervo que os predica ... —I came here with this swindler who is preaching to you now. (Chapter 5, p.69). The word *echacuervo* (scarecrow) refers to a seller of papal bulls. Today the word is a pejorative slang expression used to refer to priests. At the time the word *cuervo* (crow) was also used as a slang term to refer to the devil, thus a person who dishonestly sold papal bulls [the case of the bull seller in

Lazarillo] was called *echacuervos* as he claimed to *echar,* to rid, souls of devils.

Cervantes in *Rinconete y Cortadillo* also makes reference to this: *"mi padre es … ministro de Santa Cruzada; quiero decir que es buldero, como lo llama el vulgo, aunque otros lo llaman echacuervos"* (my father is … a minister of the Holy Crusade; I mean he's a seller of bulls, as the common man calls them, though others call them scarecrows.)

…a tercero día hacíamos Sant Juan … — … on the third day we did a St. John. (Chapter 1, p.20). The expression *hacer San Juan* is a slang term meaning to leave, or to go away. San Juan (St. John) was the patron saint of servants and it was customary that any servant who wanted to leave his master would do so on the feast of St. John. As Correas shows in his collection, at that time there were various proverbs in circulation related to San Juan, e.g.: *San Juan de los criados, cuando los mozos dejan a sus amos* (St John patron of servants, when boys leave their masters); and *Día de San Juan tres costumbres: mudar casa, amo o mozo* (There are three customs on the feast of St John: a change of house, of master or of servant).

¡Quebremos el ojo al diablo!—We'll give the devil one in the eye. (Chapter 3, p.56). This slang term is used in the context of wanting to make the devil [or one's enemy] envious by enjoying some good fortune that has come one's way.

Finally, with regard to the book and its impact, it is also interesting to note that as early as 1587 Sánchez Ballesta recorded a proverbial expression derived directly from this picaresque work: *casa de Lazarillo de Tormes*, meaning a small, gloomy house.

EL INGENIOSO HIDALGO DON QUIJOTE DE LA MANCHA

In Cervantes' *Don Quijote* the down-to-earth wisdom enshrined in adages achieves its highest literary expression. The work is a veritable treasure-trove of popular maxims, mostly emanating from the mouth of the knight's rustic squire, Sancho Panza. In *Don Quijote* proverbs are given the stamp of approval by Cervantes, the master of Spanish literature, both as literary gems and as pearls of wisdom. As we saw earlier, even the ascetic and idealistic knight himself revered the insight enveloped in adages, when, in Part I, chapter 21, he says to his squire: "It seems to me, Sancho, that there is no proverb which is not true, because they are all maxims born of experience, mother of all the sciences . . ." And towards the end of Part II, chapter 67, he repeats this assertion, again reminding Sancho of the importance of proverbs, this time underscoring their roots in long experience and ancient wisdom:

> . . . *y si no me acuerdo mal, otra vez te he dicho que los refranes son sentencias breves, sacadas de la experiencia y especulación de nuestros antiguos sabios;* . . .

> . . . and if I remember rightly, I have told you before that proverbs are brief maxims, drawn from the experience and observations of our wise old men . . .

However, immediately after uttering these words, Don Quijote cautions that proverbs must be used appropriately: " . . . *y el refrán que no viene a propósito antes es disparate que sentencia.*" (. . . and the proverb that is ill applied is not wisdom but nonsense). The following exchange between Quijote and Sancho on the role and merit of adages concerns the knight's dislike of Sancho's abuse, through over-use, of proverbial dicta. Sancho's proverbial erudition is such that he is able to call on his limitless stock of adages, and articulate them with such alacrity that instead of offering up one aptly-directed maxim, he often spouts them in litany form. This is usually done to help him express his earthy philosophy of life, or to support or refute a particular argument being put forward. In this scene (in chapter 67) Don Quijote and Sancho are discussing the merits of becoming shepherds and leading a pastoral life for a year. Mulling this over, Sancho considers that a pastoral life could also have its problems, declaring:

> *Sanchica mi hija nos llevará la comida al hato. ¡Pero guarda!, que es de buen parecer, y hay pastores más maliciosos que simples, y no querría que «fuese por lana y volviese trasquilada»; y también suelen andar los amores y los no buenos deseos por los campos como por las ciudades, y por las pastorales chozas como por los reales palacios, y «quitada la causa, se quita el pecado»; y «ojos que no ven corazón que no*

quiebra»; y «más vale salto de mata que ruego de hombres buenos».

My daughter Sanchica will bring our dinner to us in the field. But, watch out! For she is good looking, and shepherds are not all simple, some are rogues, and I would not want her «to go for wool and come back shorn». For your lovings and wanton desires are as common in the fields as in the cities, and you find them in shepherds' huts as well as in royal palaces. So «take away the opportunity and you take away the sin»; and «what the eye doesn't see the heart doesn't grieve for»; and «a leap over the hedge is better than good men's prayers».

Ojos que no ven, corazón que no quiebra/siente is a well known proverb and we looked at it earlier. The saying *Quitada la causa, se quita el pecado* is similar in meaning to another proverb commented on in the section dealing with *Lazarillo*: *La ocasión hace al ladrón* (opportunity makes a thief). Other Spanish proverbs with the same message are: *Ocasión y tentación, una misma cosa son; De la ocasión nace la tentación; Quien quita la tentación, quita el peligro; El aparejo hace el ladrón; En arca abierta, el justo peca.* The fourth proverb in Sancho's list, *Más vale salto de mata que ruego de hombres buenos*, was earlier recorded by Santillana (415), and counsels that if a person has committed an act which calls for punishment, the best policy is to flee, rather than rely on the prayers of worthy men. Clearly here Sancho is advocating that his daughter should escape before the dreadful act occurs, or in other words prevention is better than cure.

The rhetorical excess displayed in the litany of adages discharged by Sancho exasperates Don Quijote. He reminds his squire that he has often warned him to be more restrained in his use of adages, explaining that *"cualquiera de los que has dicho basta para dar a entender tu pensamiento"* (any one of them would be sufficient to explain your thought). However, the knight himself immediately falls into the same trap and cites two old saws of his own to highlight the futility of his efforts in instructing Sancho on this point, saying " . . . *«es predicar en desierto», y «castígame mi madre, y yo trómpogelas»"* (" . . . «it's like preaching in the desert», and «the more my mother beats me, the more I whip the top»"). To which Sancho gleefully replies:

Paréceme ... que vuesa merced es como lo que dicen: «Dijo la sartén a la caldera: Quítate allá, ojinegra»: estáme reprehendiendo que no diga yo refranes, y ensártalos vuesa merced de dos en dos.

Your worship reminds me of the saying that the pot called the kettle black. You chide me for quoting proverbs, then string them together in pairs yourself.

To this Quijote retorts, that at least when he employs proverbs they are to the point and and fit *como anillo en el dedo* (like a ring on the finger)—using another proverbial phrase. Thus the knight again reminds Sancho of the need to use proverbs judiciously and appositely.

In Part II, chapter 43, in the context of Don Quijote's instructing Sancho on how to be a good Governor of the promised isle, the knight insists that Sancho should be restrained in his speech and not interlard this with numerous axioms. For the essence of an effective maxim lies in its concision, thus prolixity in the number used offsets their power and validity:

... puesto que los refranes son sentencias breves, muchas veces los traes tan por los cabellos, que más parecen disparates que sentencias.

... for proverbs are brief axioms, yet you often drag them in inappropriately, when they sound more like nonsense than maxims.

Sancho acknowledges that he "knows more proverbs than a book" and that he can't help it if at times they come into his mouth all together and fight with one another to get out. It is, he says, because of this that they are not always to the point; but from now on the squire promises to take care only to use those that suit the gravity of his hoped-for office; and goes on to string together four more adages to support this:

... que «en casa llena, presto se guisa la cena»; y «quien destaja no baraja»; y «a buen salvo está el que repica»; y «el dar y el tener, seso ha menester».

... in «a well-stocked house the supper is soon cooked»; and «he that cuts does not deal the cards»; and «the man who sounds the alarm is safe»; and «giving and taking both call for good sense».

At this an exasperated Don Quijote tells Sancho ironically to carry on cramming in his proverbs, no one will stop him, for although he has been warned to show restraint in their use, he continues undeterred. Once more, Don Quijote cautions:

Mira, Sancho, no te digo yo que parece mal un refrán traído a propósito; pero cargar y ensartar refranes a troche moche hace la plática desmayada y baja.

Look, Sancho, I do not find fault with a proverb aptly used, but to load and string proverbs together any old how makes your speech heavy and vulgar.

Along the same lines, Juan de Mal Lara in his *Philosophia Vulgar,* Preamble 9 entitled *"A quantas cosas aprovecha la sciencia de los refranes"* (Of how many things does science take advantage from proverbs) says: " ... if the whole of our speech and writing is made up of proverbs, it loses its charm through excessive brightness ... Be judicious in this; because it will be an insult to many proverbs".

Don Quijote continues to instruct Sancho in the way a governor should comport himself, and as his squire is illiterate, he says that he should at least learn to sign his name. This, the servant says he can probably manage, but just in case, decides to pretend his hand is paralysed so as to get someone else to sign for him, attesting in proverbial fashion that: *Para todo hay remedio, si no es para la muerte*—There's a remedy for everything except death. (This adage found its way into the English language via translations of *Don Quijote* where it is used in Book II both here (chapter 43) and earlier in chapter 10). Sancho then resumes, employing a torrent of well-known and, on this occasion, appropriate proverbs, some of which he has used on other occasions:

... que «vendrán por lana, y volverán trasquilados»; y «a quien Dios quiere bien, la casa sabe bien»; y «las necedades del rico por sentencias pasan en el mundo» ... No, sino «haceos

miel, y paparos han moscas»; «tanto vales cuanto tienes», decía
una mi agüela; y «del hombre arraigado no te verás vengado».

. . . «let them come for wool and they'll go away shorn»; and
«whom God loves well, his house is well blest»; and «the rich
man's foolishness passes for wisdom in the world»; and . . . «make
yourself honey and the flies will suck you»; and «you're worth as
much as you've got», as my grandmother used to say; and «you
can't get revenge on a well-rooted man».

In the last proverb the word *arraigado* refers to a person who
is the possessor of *bienes raíces*, real estate, i.e. a person of
wealth. The proverb is a variation of the saying recorded by Santillana (241) *De hombre heredado no te verás vengado*.

Again, on hearing his squire's catalogue of old saws, Don Quijote invokes sixty thousand devils to take Sancho and his
proverbs, which, he warns, will bring his servant to the gallows
one day. The knight then starts to wonder how on earth a nit wit
like his squire manages to use maxims so effortlessly when he
himself, with all his learning, sweats and labours just to utter one.
Sancho explains that proverbs are all he has, they are his
hacienda, his birthright and his only wealth: "*ni otro caudal
alguno, sino refranes y más refranes*" (my only fortune is
proverbs and still more proverbs). Adding that four more have
come to him right now which fit like a glove, however, he says he
will refrain from mentioning them, for as the proverb goes: *Al
buen callar llaman Sancho*—Sage Silence in Sancho's name! To
which, as we saw earlier when looking at *El Corbacho*, Don Quijote replies that his squire is not the Sancho mentioned in the
proverb, rather he is an obstinate and graceless chatterbox. In
spite of this rebuke, curiosity gets the better of Don Quijote and he
cannot resist enquiring which are the apt proverbs that came so
quickly and artfully to Sancho's mind, since he admits that he has
been racking his own [superior] brain and he can't think of one.
Sancho immediately obliges his master citing, and even glossing, not
only the four proverbs referred to (which appear in quotes), but
throwing in two more for good measure as he glosses the others,
ending with the one that most succinctly encapsulates his point:

. . . *que «entre dos muelas cordales nunca pongas tus pulgares»,*
y «a idos de mi casa, y qué queréis con mi mujer, no hay

responder», y «si da el cántaro en la piedra, o la piedra en el
cántaro, mal para el cántaro», [. . .] que es menester que «el que
vea la mota en el ojo ajeno, vea la viga en el suyo», . . . «espan-
tóse la muerta de la degollada*»; y vuesa merced sabe muy bien
que «más sabe el necio en su casa que el cuerdo en la ajena».

. . . «don't put your thumbs between two eye-teeth», and «get out
of my house, what do you want with my wife?», and «whether
the pitcher hits the stone or the stone hits the pitcher, it's a bad
look-out for the pitcher», . . . So «he who points to the mote in
the other man's eye must see the beam in his own», . . . «the dead
woman was afraid of the one with her throat slit*»; and your worship well knows that «the fool knows more in his own house
than the wise man in another's».

(*This proverb, which appears in Santillana (443) as *Maravillóse
la muerte de la degollada*, has the same meaning as «*dijo la
sartén a la caldera, tírate allá, culinegra*»—The pot said to the
kettle, get out of my way, blackbottom).

The knight challenges the wisdom of the adage which teaches
that the fool knows more in his own house than the wise man in
another's, saying that the fool knows nothing in his own house or
in anyone else's, and he decides to leave Sancho for a lost cause on
the the question of adages, realising that his "fat little body is
nought but a sackful of proverbs and mischief".

This description of Sancho as *un costal de refranes* (a sackful
of proverbs) is clearly apt, and though much of his conversation is
merely sprinkled with adages, when the squire wants to insist on
a particular point he can, as we have seen, release a cascade of
them, each one standing as clarification or reinforcement of the
others. Even though his master rebukes him for this and calls such
verbal torrents a load of nonsense, Sancho himself is stubbornly
sure of the wisdom of his rhetorical birthright: the only patrimony
an illiterate rustic like himself could hope to inherit being the oral
tradition of his ancestors. Sancho has an unshakable faith in these
earthy doctrines, since their sound tenets have proved to be reliable guides in his own life and have, in a way, become part of his
flesh and blood.

This is made clear in the scene in Book II, chapter 19, when
Sancho overhears a group of labourers recount how the beautiful

country maid Quiteria is to be married off to a rich farmer named Camacho, instead of to the lovestruck shepherd Basilio. Sancho offers his advice, employing the apt proverb: *Cada oveja con su pareja*—Every ewe to her mate. Seeing Basilio so desconsolate, for he neither eats nor sleeps and is wasting away pining for his beloved, Sancho tries to raise his spirits, counselling him with a string of adages:

> *Dios lo hará mejor -dijo Sancho-; que «Dios que da la llaga, da la medicina»; «nadie sabe lo que está por venir»; «de aquí a mañana muchas horas hay», y «en una [hora], y aun en un momento, se cae la casa»; yo he visto llover y hacer sol, todo en un mismo punto; «tal se acuesta sano la noche, que no se puede mover otro día» . . . que «el amor— según yo he oído decir—mira con unos anteojos, que hacen parecer oro al cobre, a la pobreza riqueza, y a las lagañas perlas».*

God will find a cure -said Sancho-. For «God, who gives the wound, gives the cure». «No one knows what tomorrow will bring». «There are many hours between now and tomorrow», and «in one hour, even in a minute, the house falls down». I have seen rain and sunshine together at the same moment. «A man may go to bed well at night and next day he's not able to move» . . . For «Love—I have heard tell—looks through spectacles that make copper seem like gold, poverty like riches, and specks in the eye like pearls».

Don Quijote again becomes exasperated hearing such a torrent of proverbs, and challenges Sancho's knowledge of life. To this the squire replies that he is indeed right in what he says, it is simply because his master doesn't understand him that he takes what his squire says as nonsense. But Sancho shrugs this off, saying that at least he understands himself, and knows there was little foolishness in what he had said.

Don Quijote, however, is not always so scathing in his criticism of Sancho's use of proverbs, in fact he often praises him for his pertinent and sound proverbial wisdom. This was the case in Book II, chapter 59, when the knight, after another misfortune, loses his appetite and says he thinks he should let himself die of hunger, proclaiming that though Sancho was born to die eating, he himself was born to live dying of starvation. To this Sancho replies, while munching his food eagerly: "*no aprobará vuesa merced aquel refrán que dicen «muera Marta, y muera harta»*" (your worship will therefore not approve of the proverb which says: «Let Martha die, but die with her belly full»). The squire goes on to gloss this, saying the proverb is a particularly sound one for its encouragement of the joy of life instead of despair, and of eating until the very end that heaven has appointed for one. Sancho then persuades his master that a little food and a nap would do him the world of good. The knight follows Sancho's sound advice, thinking that at times his squire "reasoned more like a philosopher than a fool . . . ".

Again, in Book II, chapter 10, Quijote accepts that his squire can indeed use proverbs aptly and praises him for this. He then asks his squire to go and see the Lady Dulcinea and speak to her on his behalf. Sancho accepts this entreaty saying that his master's sad heart must feel as withered as a hazelnut. Trying to cheer him, Sancho tells the knight to take heart, counselling proverbially:

> . . . *que «buen corazón quebranta mala ventura», y «que donde no hay tocinos, no hay estacas»; y también se dice, «donde no se piensa, salta la liebre».*

> . . . for «a stout heart breaks bad luck»; and «where there is no bacon there are no hooks»; and they also say, «where you least expect it, out jumps the hare».

In Part II, chapter 7, Don Quijote has to acknowledge that Sancho does know how to hit the target with his proverbs, and declares that he too is able to *arrojar refranes como llovidos* (release a torrent of proverbs) when he wishes. Sancho then approaches his master saying he has been given orders by his wife to demand his salary before they leave for new adventures, and uses another rush of adages to express this:

> *Teresa dice -dijo Sancho- que «ate bien mi dedo» con vuesa merced , y que «hablen cartas y callen barbas», porque «quien destaja, no baraja», pues «más vale un toma que dos te daré». Y yo digo que «el consejo de la mujer es poco, y el que no le toma es loco».*

Teresa says, remarked Sancho, that I must «get this well tied up», and «let writing speak and beards be silent», since «he who shuffles the cards does not cut», and «one gift is worth two promises». And I say «there is little in a woman's advice, and he who doesn't take it is not very wise».

Quijote replies that Sancho is speaking pearls today, and thus encouraged the squire continues:

> . . . todos estamos sujetos a la muerte, y que «hoy somos y mañana no», y que «tan presto se va el cordero como el carnero», y que nadie puede prometerse en este mundo más horas de vida de las que Dios quisiere darle . . . En fin, yo quiero saber lo que gano, poco o mucho que sea; que «sobre un huevo pone la gallina*», y «muchos pocos hacen un mucho», y «mientras se gana algo no se pierde nada».

> . . . we are all subject to death: «here to-day and gone tomorrow», and «the lamb goes to the spit as soon as the sheep», and nobody can promise himself a longer life than God wishes to grant him . . . and I should like to know how much it will be, whether it's little or much, for «the hen sits on one egg*», and «many a little makes a mickle», and «while you're earning, you're losing nothing».

*This proverb, *sobre un huevo pone la gallina*, refers to the old custom of setting down a fake egg for a hen to sit on. This was done so as to stimulate the egg-laying instinct. Thus the proverb teaches that a job or task is better executed if some stimulus or encouragement is provided.

The knight can do nothing against this proverbial barrage, and tells Sancho that he is well aware at what target he is aiming the arrows of his proverbs. But Don Quijote informs his squire that it is not proper for a knight errant to pay his squire before an adventure, and he employs the same proverbial weapons as Sancho to argue his point:

> . . . y advertid, hijo, que «vale más buena esperanza que ruin posesión», y «buena queja que mala paga». Hablo de esta manera, Sancho, por daros a entender que también como vos sé yo arrojar refranes como llovidos; . . .

. . . And remember this, son, «good hopes are better than poor possessions», and «a good claim is better than bad pay». I speak in this way, Sancho, to show you that I can rain down proverbs as well as you . . .

As mentioned, Sancho is regarded as *el padre de los proverbios*, the father of proverbs; maxims being his only possessions and the sole legacy he had to pass on to his children. A particularly memorable scene referring to Sancho's prodigious proverbial knowledge is in Book II, chapter 50, when the Duke and Duchess's young page comes to visit Sancho's wife, Teresa, and their daughter, Sanchica, to inform them of Sancho's recent good fortune in being made governor of an isle. On hearing this, Sanchica remarks on what she believes the villagers' reaction will be when they see that she has gone up in the world. She is sure they will comment:

Mirad la tal por cual, hija del harto de ajos, y como va sentada y tendida en el coche, como si fuera una papesa. Pero pisen ellos los lodos, y ándeme yo en mi coche levantados lo pies del suelo. Mal año y mal mes para cuantos murmuradores hay en el mundo; y «ándeme yo caliente y ríase la gente». ¿Digo bien, madre mía?.

Look at that so and so, daughter of the old garlic bag, see how she sits there and lolls about in that coach, just like some she-pope. But let them trudge through the mud, while I ride in my coach with my feet up. A bad year and a worse month to all the scandalmongers in the world, «so long as I go warm let them scoff». Is that not right, mother?

Sanchica's mother, Teresa, replies that her daughter is absolutely right, and quotes Sancho and his proverbial pearls to prove it:

Y como yo he oído decir muchas veces a tu buen padre (que así como lo es tuyo lo es de los refranes), «cuando te dieren la vaquilla, corre con soguilla»; cuando te dieren un gobierno, cógele; cuando te dieren un condado, agárrale; y cuando te hicieren tus tus con alguna buena dádiva, envásala.

As I've often heard your good father say—who just as he is yours, so is he the father of proverbs,—«when they give you a calf, make haste with the halter»; when they give you a governorship, take hold of it; when they give you an earldom, grab it; and when they slip you a good gift, pocket it.

Sanchica declares she doesn't care if people call out "*«vióse el perro en bragas de cerro», y lo demás.*" ("«look there at the dog in a doublet!», and all the rest.") when they see her stuck up and showing off. The proverbial phrase used here by Sanchica is the first part of the adage: *Vióse el perro en bragas de cerro y no conoció a su compañero*; meaning: once a person has gone up in the world, he or she does not want to recognise former companions. The proverb was recorded earlier in *El Corbacho* (108) and in *Refranes que dicen las viejas* (710).

On hearing Sanchicas's words, the local priest, who was standing along side the group, remarks to the duchess's page that he cannot help thinking but that the whole tribe of Panzas were born with their bellies stuffed with proverbs, for they come out with them at every turn. The page agrees, saying Sancho uses them continually and though they are not always to the point, the Lady Duchess commends them highly.

When Sanchica asks the page to take her to see her father on the back of his horse, he informs her that the daughters of governors should not travel the highways alone and mounted on horses, but in carriages with a large number of servants. To this Sanchica retorts that she can journey as well upon an ass as in a carriage. But her mother intervenes, and explains to her daughter that the page is right in what he says for, as the proverb says: " . . . *«tal el tiempo, tal el tiento»: cuando Sancho, Sancha, y cuando gobernador, señora . . .* ". (. . . «other days, other ways»—when Sancho, it was Sancha, and when governor, my Lady . . .).

For Sancho and his family proverbs are the daily bread of conversation, their stock-in-trade. And despite Don Quijote's advice to his squire not to abuse adages by overuse, but to employ them judiciously and appropriately, neither Sancho nor his family find it possible to speak otherwise. This oral tradition constitutes an important part of their patrimony: it is the source of their homespun wisdom, and often their only consolation in life. Their proverbial wealth is the inheritance bequeathed by their forefathers.

This is reflected once more, at the end of the book (chapter

71). Here the two adventurers decide to return home, but Sancho does not want to go back penniless. He thus explains to his master why he (Sancho) should not delay scourging himself with a whip (for which Don Quijote has promised his squire money—*un cuartillo* for each lash), and releases four more proverbs to back up his explanation:

> ...*porque* «*en la tardanza suele estar muchas veces el peligro*»; *y* «*a Dios rogando y con el mazo dando*»; *y que* «*más valía un toma que dos te daré*»; *y* «*el pájaro en la mano que el buitre volando*».

> ... because «danger often lurks in delay»; and «God helps those who help themselves»; and «one gift is worth more than two promises»; and «a bird in the hand is worth more than a vulture in flight».

Sancho continues to string proverbs together willy-nilly, causing Don Quijote to exclaim "*No más refranes, Sancho, por un solo Dios*" (No more proverbs, Sancho, for God's sake). He tells his squire that if he speaks plainly and clearly and without interlacing his language he will see that "*vale un pan por ciento*" (one loaf will be worth a hundred).

To this Sancho responds that he doesn't know how to reason without using proverbs, or how to use a proverb that doesn't ring true. He tells his master that he would mend his ways if he could, but of course his problem—and his charm—is that he can't. Proverbs are of his essence, his belly is stuffed with them, and just as the biblical Ethiopian cannot change his skin, or the leopard his spots,[42] nor can Sancho change the nature of his speech.

VII

Sayings of Yesterday and Today
A Rich and Colourful Legacy

1. NAMES OF PEOPLE AND PLACES IN POPULAR SAYINGS

We have already seen some examples of the way names of people and places form part of well-known sayings. In some cases, the origin of the phrase and the identity of the person or place are known and can be traced back to colourful characters, historical events, or local customs and beliefs. There are many other cases, however, where this information has long since been lost and where the original reference can only be guessed at from the meaning the phrase or idiom now carries. Examples of both the above cases are shown here below:

[Darse el] Abrazo de Vergara—Lit: [To give each other the] Embrace of Vergara; meaning: To make it up; Let bygones be bygones. This saying is rooted in the historical event of the Agreement—reached in Vergara on 31 August 1839, between the Carlist and Liberal armies which marked the end of the 1ST Carlist War.

A cada puerco le llega su San Martín—St Martin's day arrives for every pig; meaning: Everyone gets their come-uppance/just deserts in the end. As seen earlier, this proverb alludes to the festival of San Martín, celebrated around 11TH November, a time when it was, and in some areas still remains, the custom in Spain to slaughter pigs in order to prepare pork and ham products for the year.

Al buen callar llaman Sancho—Sage Silence is Sancho's name. This proverb counsels moderation and discretion in speech. The origin of the saying is uncertain though it is thought that Sancho was a common name used in old colloquial Spanish for *santo* (saint), or *bueno* (good). This is seen in *Corbacho* (220) where it appears as: *A buen callar llaman santo*—Silence is saintly/good, which again has a similar meaning to: Silence is golden, a proverb found in many languages.

Alcalde de Monterilla, ¡ay de aquel que por su acera pilla!— Lit: Mayor of Monterilla, woe betide the person he finds on his pavement! *Monterilla* is a colloquial name for *alcalde* (mayor). This rather paradoxical idiom is used to denote a person who, once in authority, becomes dictatorial and gives unreasonable/ absurd orders, or does preposterous things. The phrase has its origin in the local tale of the Mayor of Dos Hermanas, a town near Seville. Apparently, around the time of the so-called *Goloriosa* Revolution in September 1868, the then mayor championed the love of two young villagers by marrying them, against the wishes of the girl's father. When the father found out, he confronted the mayor asserting furiously that the only valid marriage was one instituted by God and the Council of Trent. To which the autocratic mayor replied: "In that case, from this instant I declare the Council of Trent annulled." Nowadays, the idiom more commonly used in Andalusia is: *Como el alcalde de Dos Hermanas*.

Algo va de Pedro a Pedro—Lit: Something goes from Peter to Peter; a phrase used to stress the differences that exists between two people.

¡Alza/Arsa la Pepa!—Andalusian exclamation used to express surprise or incredulity. *Pepa* is the colloquial form of the name Josefa. See also *¡Viva la Pepa!* below.

(Los) Amantes de Teruel, tonta ella y tonto él—Lit: The lovers of Teruel, foolish she and foolish he. It refers to the story of the young couple from Teruel, Diego Martínez de Marcilla and Isabel

de Segura, who were forced by ill-luck to live apart. The saying is thought to have its origin in the fabled heroes from the work by Boccacio, entitled *Girolamo and Salvestra*. The legend was later recounted by Pérez de Montalbán and Tirso de Molina. During the Spanish Romantic period the tale was revived by J.E. Hartzenbusch in his dramatic work *Los amantes de Teruel*. The couples' supposed remains are preserved in the church of San Pedro, Teruel.

Andar como las vacas del Tío Meleno—To wander like Uncle Meleno's cows; meaning: Unruly; To be all over the place; To be a rule unto oneself.

¡Anda y que te mate El Tato!—Lit: Go and may *El Tato* kill you. Andalusian idiom meaning: Get lost!, Push off!, Give me a break!, Leave me in peace!, etc. *El Tato* was the nickname of Antonio Sánchez, a famous bull fighter of the mid-1800s who was renowned for his prowess in killing bulls rapidly and cleanly. Other similar expressions are: *Anda y que te mate El Tato y te morirás de gusto*—Lit: Go and may El Tato kill you, and you will die a pleasant death; *A ese no le mata ni El Tato*—Not even El Tato can kill him.

Año de la Quica [del siglo de la polca/del catapún]—Year of la Quica [in the century of the polka/ the year dot]; meaning: Ancient; Very old.

Aquí morirá Sansón con todo los filisteos—Lit: Here will die Samson with the all Philistines. Expression indicating the imperative that all risks and dangers must be braved.

Armarse la de San Quintín—To cause/create that of St. Quintin; meaning: To cause a terrible row/a lot of trouble. Alludes to the Battle of 1557, during the reign of Philip II, when the Spanish army defeated the French at St Quintin on 10TH August, the feast of San Lorenzo. To commemorate this victory Philip II ordered the Monastery of San Lorenzo El Escorial to be built.

Averígüelo Vargas—Let Vargas find out/do it. There are myriad theories as to the origin of this old saying. Gracián in *El Criticón* (III, 10) mentions that the phrase was used by Ferdinand the Catholic King whenever a problem was brought to his attention.

In his *Tesoro*, Covarrubias states that the Vargas referred to was one Francisco de Vargas, secretary to King Ferdinand, a man of outstanding intellect, and in whom the King had great confidence. Because of this, Vargas was charged by the King with investigating most of the difficult problems that were placed before the monarch.

Bien canta Marta cuando está harta—Martha sings well with her belly full.

(Las) Bodas de Camacho—Lit:The wedding feast of Camacho. This refers to the scene of the wedding celebration mentioned in Cervantes' novel *Don Quijote* (Book II, chs. 20 and 21), and the idiom is now used to describe a large reception/banquet/dinner.

(La) Carabina de Ambrosio—Lit: Ambrosio's carbine rifle. Andalusian expression used to refer to something useless or ineffective. It alludes to an antihero of Andalusian folklore, who lived in Seville in the early 1800s. The story goes that Ambrosio was a farm labourer who could not make a living in the fields and so decided to become a bandit. To this end, he prepared his trusty rifle, loaded with bullets from which the gunpowder had been removed. However, his naivety was so renowned that each time he attempted a highway robbery his victims simply ignored his threats and laughed at him. Thus the failed highwayman was forced to return to his former labours, blaming his useless rifle for his lack of success.

(La) Casa de Tócame Roque—The house of Tócame Roque; meaning: A riotous, rowdy, disorderly place. The saying refers to a house in Madrid in a street called *Barquillo*. The house, which was renowned for brawls and general rowdy behaviour was demolished in the mid-1800s. However, it served as the inspiration for the writer Ramón de la Cruz's farce entitled *La Petra y la Juana o el buen casero*, and accordingly the play was more commonly known as *La casa de Tócame Roque*.

Como Dios pintó a Perico—As God painted Perico; Andalusian idiom meaning: effortlessly; piece of cake; cinch. Perico is a colloquial name for Pedro (Peter).

Como el alcalde de Dos Hermanas—Like the Mayor of Dos Hermanas. See *Alcalde de Monterilla* above.

Como el alcalde de Ronquillo—Like the Mayor of Ronquillo. Idiom denoting a jocular, waggish sort of person. Ronquillo is a village in the province of Seville.

Como el alcalde de Trebujena [que se murió de sentir penas ajenas]—Like the Mayor of Trebujena [who died of the sorrows of others]. Trebujena is a village in the province of Cádiz. The idiom denotes a person who becomes preoccupied with other people's concerns. Another version is: *Como el cura de Trebujena, que murió de sentir penas ajenas*—Like the priest of Trebujena, who died of the sorrows of others.

Como el gaitero de Bujalance [un maravedí por que empiece y diez por que acabe]—Like the piper of Bujalance [one maravedí (old Spanish coin) for him to start and ten for him to stop]. A saying used to refer to people who let a little success or ability go to their heads and become over-confident or conceited—once they start, it is difficult to get them to stop. Bujalance is a village in the province of Córdoba.

Como la purga de Benito—Like Benito's purgative; meaning: Having a rapid effect; Also refers to the impatient who cannot wait for desired results. This alludes to the anecdote about the legendary Benito, who, while still in the pharmacy found that the laxative he had been prescribed was already taking effect.

Como los novios de Hornachuelos, que él lloraba por no llevarla y ella por no ir con él—Like the Sweethears of Hornachuelos, he cried not to take her and she not to go with him. This is a saying that emphasizes disharmony or incompatibility between two people. The phrase has its origin in a wedding that was arranged without the consent or knowledge of a young couple in the village of Hornachuelos in the province of Córdoba.

Como Mateo con la guitarra—Like Mateo with his guitar; meaning: With great care and attention; to treat something with kid gloves.

Como Pedro por su casa—Like Pedro round his house; meaning: As if you/he owned the place. In Aragón the saying often takes the form: *Entrarse como Pedro por Huesca*—To enter like Pedro in Huesca (alluding to the conquest of Huesca by Pedro I of Aragón in 1094.)

Como Periquillo Sarmiento que fue a cagá y se lo llevó er viento—Like Periquillo Sarmiento who went to shit and the wind blew him away. In Andalusia, the letter *l* is sometimes pronounced as *r*, thus *er viento* means *el viento* (the wind). This saying is an Andalusian version of: *Como Mari-Sarmiento que fue a cagar y llevola el viento*. Cejador in his work *Fraseología o Estilística castellana* records that the name Mari-Sarmiento was the slang term for a skinny woman—as thin as a vine shoot [*sarmiento*]. Thus the saying is used to denote an extremely thin person.

Como Quevedo, que ni sube, ni baja, ni se está quedo—Like Quevedo, who neither goes up nor down, nor remains still. This idiom is used to indicate that someone is in difficulty yet is unable to overcome it and consequently causes problems or uneasiness for everyone else around. The phrase is attributed to the writer Francisco de Quevedo and one of his amorous assignations. The circumstances are reminiscent of the trick played on Falstaff by Mistresses Ford and Page when, in his assignation with the former (Act 3, scene II of *The Merry Wives of Windsor*), Falstaff was forced to hide in a buck-basket; and also the anecdote about Virgil, who was left in a basket hanging from a tower, as recounted in *Libro de Buen Amor, Corbacho* and *Celestina*. In the case of Quevedo, the maiden concerned set about making a fool of him by calling out to him from a balcony and suggesting that he get into a tub, which she and a servant would then pull up to the balcony. Quevedo naively obliged, and when the tub was halfway up, the maiden, with he help of a group of revellers (who were hiding behind the balcony) left him swinging in mid-air. They then proceeded to barrack insults and sarcastic remarks at the famous writer, which he returned in good measure. When the night patrol arrived and asked "Who's there?", Quevedo replied: "*Quevedo, que ni sube, ni baja, ni se está quedo.*"

Como quien tiene un tío en Alcalá/América [que ni tiene un tío ni tiene ná]—Like the one who has an uncle in Alcala/America [he has neither uncle nor anything else]. Phrase used to refer to someone you suspect is inventing things about himself or family in order to impress.

Como San Jinojo en el cielo—Like St. Jinojo in heaven; meaning: ignored by all/not known. The name of this would-be saint (Jinojo) does not appear in the Collections of the lives of the saints and thus he is unknown, or does not exist.

(El) Corral de la Pacheca—Lit: The courtyard of Pacheca; meaning: A noisy and riotous place. The saying alludes to a court-yard in a street called *calle Príncipe* in Madrid, where theatrical works were put on in the mid-sixteenth century. The owner of the courtyard was one Isabel Pacheco, known as La Pacheca.

¡Corta, Blas, que no me vas!—Cut it, Blas, I won't swallow it! Phrase used to stop someone from continuing to talk; some-thing akin to: Cut the crap. See also: *Lo dijo Blas, punto redondo*, below.

(Las) Cuentas del Gran Capitán—The accounts of the Great Captain; meaning: Excessively expensive, exorbitant costs; also: Lacking proper proof or receipts. *El Gran Capitán* was the epi-thet given to Gonzalo Fernández de Córdoba (1453–1515), a renowned warrior who fought on the side of the Catholic Mon-archs, defeating the Moors in the conquest of Granada in 1492, and who led the Spanish army in the conquest of the Kingdom of Naples, of which he was named Viceroy. It is thought that *las cuentas* mentioned in the saying alludes to the request by the Catholic Monarchs for the soldier to provide them with precise accounts, showing all costs incurred in the battles for the con-quest of Naples. The Captain is said to have become indignant at this 'unreasonable' demand, complaining that the king had asked for accounts from one who had given him a kingdom. However, when the Captain eventually presented the accounts, these proved to be excessive and showed that the soldier had seemingly spent much more than he had received.

Chuminada de la [tía] Carlota—Idiocy/Inanity of [aunt] Car-lota. Andalusian saying used to denote foolishness, asininity, sense-lessness of some form.

De Matute—[In the way] of Matute; meaning: To do something on the sly; In a secret manner; Smuggle. A popular Andalusian folk song runs:

A lo contrabandista	Like a contrabandist
tengo que amarte:	I must love you:
que si no es de Matute,	For if not done secretly
no puedo hablarte.	I can't speak to you.

De Rodríguez—[In the way] of Rodríguez. Rodríguez is a common Spanish surname. The expression *de Rodríguez* is used to describe the situation of a husband who, while his wife is away or stays at home, is able to enjoy the life of a single man.

Después de Dios, la casa de Quirós—After God, Quiros's house. Idiom used to denote arrogance. The expression has its origin in an Asturian heraldic motto.

¿Dónde va Vicente? Donde va la gente—Where's Vincent going? Where everyone else goes; meaning: To follow the herd; someone who is easily led. Another expression employing the name Vicente is: *En casa del tío Vicente*—In uncle Vincent's house; meaning: A popular place; place frequented by many. This forms the first line of a once-popular folk song, the second line of which makes the meaning of the idiom clear. These lines run:

En casa del tío Vicente	In uncle Vincent's house
hay mucha gente.	There's a lot of people.

It is thought that the folk song is rooted in the old anecdote about a baker named Vicente, from the village of Alcuéscar (in the province of Cáceres) who hired out his home for village dances.

Durar más que la obra del Pilar—To take longer than the work on El Pilar. This Aragonese saying is used to indicate that a matter or a piece of work is taking an inordinate length of time. It alludes to the church of Our Lady of Pilar, in Zaragoza, on which work commenced in 1689, and continues still.

¡Echa el freno, Magdaleno!—Put on the brake, Magdaleno; meaning: Calm down; Calm your anger.

El que quiera higos de Lepe, que trepe—If you want figs from Lepe, climb [for them]; meaning: If you want something, you must be prepared to work for it. Lepe is a village in the province of Huelva, southern Spain, and is famous for its figs and other fruits. Many of the early expeditions to the New World set out from the ports of Huelva, and figs were an important part of the food provisions, being one of the few fruits suitable for long voyages as they could be dried.

En Baeza, tanto valen los pies como la cabeza—In Baeza, feet are worth as much as the head. This is a saying used to ridicule the conceit of those who have too high an opinion of themselves. It is derived from the story of a noble man from Baeza (in the Andalusian province of Jaén) who decided to have a pair of shoes made from a velvet cap. These he then wore on his walks through the town, and on seeing the surprise registered by his neighbours he replied arrogantly: "*En Baeza, tanto valen los pies como la cabeza*".

En la calle de Meca, quien no entra no peca—Who doesn't enter Meca Street, doesn't sin. This idiom counsels that it is better to stay away from temptation. It alludes to a once-famous street in Zaragoza which was the gathering place of prostitutes.

En los brazos de Morfeo—In the arms of Morpheus; meaning: Asleep.

En tiempos de Maricastaña—In the days of Maricastaña; meaning: A long time ago; In remote antiquity. There are many theories as to the possible origin of this saying and the legendary personage Maricastaña. Correas in his *Vocabulario* states that it refers to remote and ignorant times, when any absurd assertion was possible, a time when animals, fish and trees spoke. Cervantes uses the phrase in his exemplary novel *El casamiento engañoso* (The Deceitful Marriage), where it appears as *En tiempos de Maricastaña, cuando hablaban las calabazas* (In the days of Maricastaña when pumpkins spoke). Another hypothesis is that the name is derived from the word *casta* (pure/chaste) and thus meant a chaste or pure woman (Maria)—enclosed and protected within a shell, like a *castaña*, or chestnut. Yet another theory suggests that the name alludes to a certain Mari-Castaña who lived in Lugo is the

XIV century and who, along with other members of her family, led the insurrection against the payment of tithes imposed by the local bishop.

Esa ya va para Carmona—That's now going towards Carmona. This Andalusian idiom is used to indicate that a storm is abating or moving on. *Esa* means *esa tormenta* (that storm). This saying is employed mainly in the area around Seville, in whose province Carmona is found. It is thought that, as it is often the case in areas of Andalusia for the letter *l* to be pronounced as *r*, the phrase plays on the similarity between the words *Carmona* and *calmona* (from *calma*, calm), thus indicating that the storm is now calming.

Estar entre Pinto y Valdemoro—Lit: To be between Pinto and Valdemoro; meaning: Unable to make up one's mind between two things or opinions; Not to know what to do; Also: To be half drunk. Pinto and Valdemoro are two villages near Madrid, separated by a stream. It is thought that the origin of the saying is the tale of a man from Pinto who was usually to be found in an inebriated state. In the evenings he would go down to the stream with his friends and amuse himself by jumping from one side of the stream to the other, saying "Now I am in Pinto, now I am in Valdemoro". One day while doing this, he fell into the stream and exclaimed: "Now I'm between Pinto and Valdemoro!"

¡Esto es Jauja!—This is heaven!; The Promised Land; The land of milk and honey; This is the life! The saying has its origin in a XVI century theatrical sketch by Lope de Rueda, entitled *La tierra de Jauja*. This tells the story of Mendrugo, a simple peasant, who, as he was taking food to his wife in prison, was stopped by two con men. They started to dazzle the poor man with tales of the land of Jauja: an island of gold, beauty and happiness, whose streets are paved with egg yolk, and where the rivers flow with milk, the mountains give cheese and the trees give sweet buns. As the man stood dreaming of such wonders, the two rogues stole the food he was carrying.

[Como los de] Fuenteovejuna, todos a una—[Like those from] Fuenteovejuna, all together. This saying denotes an act of solidarity by a group of people in order to achieve a common end.

The phrase was immortalized in Lope de Vega's play *Fuenteove-juna*. The saying and the play are rooted in an actual event that took place on 23 April 1476 in the village of *Fuenteovejuna*, province of Córdoba. The story relates how the villagers were tyrannized by the feudal Fernán Gómez de Guzmán, Commander of the Knighthood of Calatrava, who, among other things, demanded the villagers pay high taxes, subjected them to ill-treatment and humiliation, and forced the village women to submit to his sexual demands. The villagers, unable to take any more of his vile treatment, decided to take justice into their own hands. On the day mentioned, they stormed the Commander's palace and killed him together with his servants. They then threw his corpse into the street and cut it to pieces. When the judge sent by the Catholic Monarchs arrived to investigate and try the case, he asked each villager in turn who had done the terrible deed, only to receive the same reply every time: "*Fuenteovejuna*".

Habla más que Castelar en el Congreso—He/she talks more than Castelar in Congress/Parliament; meaning: To be long-winded; A chatterbox. The phrase refers to the well-known politician, orator and writer Emilio Castelar y Ripoll (1832-99).

Hacer un San Miguel—To do a St Michael; meaning: To hit/punch someone violently. The idiom alludes to the Archangel mentioned in the Book of Revelations, who vanquished the devil with his mighty sword, sending him into hell.

Hacerse el Lorenzo/el longui—Lit: To do the Lorenzo/the longui. This Andalusian expression means to feign distraction.

(El) Huevo de Colón—Columbus' egg; meaning: All that was previously thought to be impossible until someone proves the contrary. This alludes to the anecdote recounted about Columbus' plans to find a new route to the Indies, which most learned men of the time thought impossible. However when he discovered the New World, the very same men said his achievement was not so outstanding. In order to deride their attitude and make them look foolish, Columbus challenged them to try and make a boiled egg stand upright. All replied that the request was impossible to achieve. Columbus then tapped the egg on the tabletop, slightly denting and flattening one end of the shell, then promptly placed

the egg on the table in an upright position. The onlookers again said that this was an obvious solution, and Columbus replied: "Yes, but none of you was able to think of it before." Calderón de la Barca also recounts a similar happening in his play *La Dama Duende*, when he mentions the *huevo de Juanelo*, recounting how a famous architect, Juanelo, carried out seemingly impossible plans to make the waters of the river Tajo reach the highest point in Toledo.

Irse por los cerros de Ubeda—To go off into the hills of Ubeda; meaning: To go off at a tangent; To wander off track verbally; Out of context. There are many theories as to the origin of this saying. One of the most colourful is that it refers to the mayor of an Andalusian village in the mountain range of Ubeda (province of Jaén). It seems that the mayor was madly in love with a young girl who lived on one of the hillsides, and would visit often. One day, during a council meeting on a particular subject, the mayor began to go off at a tangent. After a while one the villagers attending the meeting interrupted him saying: "*No se vaya usía por los cerros de Ubeda*" (Your Lordship, don't wander off into the hills of Ubeda).

[Ser un] Juan Lanas—Lit: [To be] a Juan Lanas; meaning: A man of little character or back-bone. The word *lana* means wool, and could thus be a metaphor for a soft, unclear, woolly sort of person. The name Juan is used in many Spanish sayings and is associated with an easy-going, long-suffering person, or someone who is slightly dim-witted. Some other idioms employing the name Juan are:

Juan de la Torre, a quien la baba le corre—Juan de la Torre, who dribbles saliva.

Juan Topete, que se metía a luchar con siete—Juan Topete, who got into a fight with seven.

Dos Juanes y un Pedro hacen un asno entero—Two Juans and one Pedro make one complete ass.

Juan Palomo: yo me lo guiso y yo me lo como—Juan Palomo, I cook it, I eat it. Idiom used to denote a person who keeps everything for himself or his group, ignoring the needs or existence of others. *Palomo* is a Spanish surname and also the word for cock-pigeon.

Lo dijo Blas, punto redondo—Blas said it, full stop. Meaning: There's nothing more to be said on the matter. Saying used to refer to a person who believes or boasts that he/she is always right. The phrase is thought to have its origin in the tale of a feudal lord named Blas who was renowned for his autocratic rule. When arbitrating on questions or conflicts between his subjects and pronouncing in favour of one, the other/s would often protest. Blas would then dismiss the latter, who would invariably slide way muttering: "*Lo dijo Blas, punto redondo*".

Los que a Sodoma se pasan, cuando les asen, los asan—Those who move to Sodom, when they are caught, they are cooked. This saying refers to the royal decree, issued by the Catholic Monarchs in 1497, against homosexuality. The decree ruled that the sodomite, after being hanged, should be burnt at the stake.

(El) Maestro Ciruela/de Siruela, que no sabe leer y pone escuela—Schoolmaster Ciruela/of Siruela, who couldn't read but set up a school. Ironic saying, that scoffs as those who talk or give lectures on things of which they ignorant. Siruela is a village in the province of Badajoz, in Extremedura, western Spain. There are other versions of this idiom, mentioning different localities. For example:

El maestro de Algodor, que no sabía leer y daba lección—The schoolmaster of Algodor, who couldn't read but gave classes.

El maestro de Campillo, que no sabía leer y tomaba niños— The schoolmaster of Campillo, who couldn't read and took children [as pupils].

Más años/viejo que Matusalén/Maricastaña—As old as Methuselah/Maricastaña; meaning: Very old; From ancient antiquity. (See also: *En tiempos de Maricastaña* above).

Más basto que la Bernarda [que se bajaba las bragas a pedos]—Coarser than Bernarda [who pulled down her pants farting].

Más desgraciado que el Pupas—More unfortunate than Pupas; meaning: Bad luck. *Pupas* is a word used by children to express pain or bruising.

Más feo/listo/viejo que el Carracuca—Uglier/cleverer/older than Carracuca. Carracuca is a fictitious personage whose name is used in popular sayings.

Más feo que Picio—As ugly as Picio; meaning: As ugly as sin. Sbarbi recounts that Picio was the name of a shoemaker from Alhendín, who lived in Granada in the early 1900s. He was sentenced to death, then pardoned, just minutes before the appointed time of execution. The shock of this was such that he lost his hair, eyebrows and eyelashes, and his face broke out in sores. His appearance was so horrendous that his name has since been associated with ugliness. In Andalusia another popular comparison for ugliness is: *Más feo que el sargento de Utrera*—Uglier than the Sergeant from Utrera (a village in the province of Seville).

Más fuerte era Sansón y lo venció el amor—Samson was stronger and love defeated him.

Más listo que Cardona/Merlín/Lepe—Cleverer than Cardona/Merlin/Lepe. Cardona refers to the Viscount of Cardona, friend of Prince Don Fernando, who in 1363 was executed by his brother King Pedro IV of Aragón (known as Pedro the Cruel). Cardona escaped the killing, fleeing from Castellón to Cardona.

Merlin is the famed magician of Arthurian legend, whose name appeared in many novels of knight errantry, and who was renowned for his cunning. According to popular belief, his father was the devil. Cervantes refers to this in his *Quijote* (II, chs. 23 and 35). In chapter 23 he writes:

> *Merlin, aquel francés encantador que dicen que fue hijo del diablo; y lo que yo creo es que no fue hijo del diablo, sino que supo, como dicen, un punto más que el diablo.*
> Merlin, that French wizard, who, they say, was the devil's son; though I believe he was not the son of the devil, but rather, as the saying goes, knew one trick more than the devil.

Lepe refers to don Pedro de Lepe y Dirantes, the eminent bishop of Calahorra y Calzada, born in 1641 in Sanlúcar de Barrameda. He was renowned for his great intellect and erudition.

Más ingenioso que Don Quijote—More ingenious than Don Quijote. This alludes to the full title of Cervantes' novel: *El Ingenioso Hidalgo Don Quijote de la Mancha.*

Más rumboso que Pedro Lacamba—More generous/ostentatious than Pedro Lacamba. Pedro Lacamba was a renowned smuggler, who was the subject of many flamenco songs. This saying is much used in the province of Huelva.

Más seco que el ojo de Benito—Drier than Benito's eye; (similar to: *Más seco que un ojo de un tuerto*—Drier than the [blind eye] of a one-eyed man). Two rather macabre idioms both denoting a very thin person; also means: To be broke, destitute.

Más tieso/seco que la pata de Perico—Stiffer/drier than Perico's leg. Andalusian saying referring to a certain Perico who had a wooden leg.

Muera Marta, y muera harta—Let Martha die with her belly full.

No morirá Curro de cornada de burro—Curro will not die from the horn of a donkey. Idiom used to mock cowards. Curro is the familiar name for Francisco.

No se ganó Zamora en una hora—Zamora wasn't won in an hour; meaning: Rome wasn't built in a day. This alludes to the 7 month siege of Zamora in 1072, when King Sancho el Bravo (The Brave), attempted to take Zamora from his sister, Doña Urraca. The king was eventually killed by Bellido Dolfos.

Ponerse como el Quico/como un Pepe—Lit: To become like el Quico/ like a Pepe; meaning: To eat a great amount, overindulge.

Por guasón ahorcaron a Ravenga, y después de ahorcado sacaba la lengua—For waggery they hanged Ravenga, and afterwards he stuck out his tongue. A macabre saying which underscores the recalcitrant attitude of the obstinate, who refuse to be put down by any punishment.

Puntual como un Pepe—As punctual as a Pepe; meaning: Very punctual.

Quedarse como el gallo de Morón [sin plumas y cacareando]—To be left like the Cock of Morón [featherless and cackling]; meaning: The conceited and arrongant always come to a bad end. There are many opinions regarding the origin of this saying. One is that it refers to the end suffered by a despotic governor of Morón (a town in the province of Seville) in XVI century, whose tyranny led to him being assassinated.

Another is that it refers to an arrogant law officer who, in XVI century, was charged with bringing order to the unruly town, and who declared that in Morón he was the only *gallo* (cock). His fate was sealed when one night a group of influential townspeople abducted him and took him to a road outside the town, here they stripped and whipped him, and told him to leave town or he would meet an even worse fate.

Yet another version is that the saying refers to a tax collector who was left "stripped and cackling" by the townsfolk, when he tried to collect taxes from them.

¡Que lo haga Rita [la Cantaora]!—Let Rita [the flemenco singer] do it!; meaning: Refusal to do something.

¡Que si quieres arroz, Catalina!—Do you want rice, Catalina? This is a saying that underscores the difficulty or impossibility of achieving something. It alludes to the anecdote about a certain Catalina, who lived in Sahagún at the time of Juan II of Castile, in the first half of the XV century. The woman not only loved eating rice, but also recommended it as a cure for all ills. When she fell dangerously ill herself, all her visitors asked her the same question: "Do you want rice, Catalina?", but the woman died without being able to respond.

Quien se fue a Sevilla, perdió su silla—He who went to Seville, lost his chair/seat. Idiom that counsels caution in neglecting one's duties through absence, which can have unpleasant consequences. The saying has its origin in an ecclesiastic episode that took place during the reign of Enrique IV. The Archbishop of Seville at the time was Don Alonso de Fonseca, one of whose nephews was appointed Archbishop of Santiago de Compostela in Galicia—a difficult post as the Kingdom of Galicia was in turmoil at the time. Because of this, Fonseca, Archbishop of Seville, was asked by his nephew for help in pacifying the region. This Fonseca agreed to, on condition that the nephew replace him in Seville in the interim. When Fonseca had eventually managed to pacify Galicia and wanted to return to his post, his nephew refused to leave the see in Seville. The bitter ecclesiastical conflict that ensued was only resolved via a Papal order and the intercession of the King. The end result was that Fonseca finally regained his see, and the nephew and his followers were hanged.

Saber más que Briján/Lepe—To be more clever than Briján/ Lepe. The legendary Briján or Bricán was a wizard in the manner of Merlin. For Lepe see: *Más listo que Lepe* above.

Santa Rita, Santa Rita, lo que se da no se quita—St. Rita, St. Rita, once you give something, you can't take it back. This rhyme is used in a light-hearted way, and often by children, to underscore one's ownership of, or entitlement to, something. The saying is said to have its origin in the chant to St. Rita of Cassia by a certain maiden (renowned for her ugliness) when she lost her betrothed—whom St. Rita had managed to give her after great effort on the saint's part.

¡Santiago, y cierra, España!—St. James, attack, Spain! This is a Spanish battle cry, by which the person commends himself to St. James, and prepares to attack/defend, for the sake of Spain. St. James the apostle is the patron of Spain. The saying appears in *Quijote*, Book II, ch.58, where its meaning is made clear to the inquisitive Sancho when he asks:

> . . . *y querría que vuesa merced me dijese qué es la causa porque dicen los españoles cuando quieren dar alguna batalla, invocando aquel San Diego Matamoros: «¡Santiago, y cierra España!» ¿Está por ventura España abierta, y de modo que es menester cerrarla, o qué ceremonia es ésta?*

. . . and I'd like your worship to tell me why Spaniards, when they're going into battle, call on St James, the Moor-killer: «St James, and close Spain.» Is Spain perhaps open so that she has to be closed? or what is this ceremony"

Simplicísimo eres, Sancho, respondió don Quijote; y mira que este gran caballero de la cruz bermeja háselo dado Dios a España por patrón y amparo suyo, especialmente en los rigurosos trances que con los moros los españoles han tenido, y así le invocan y llaman como a defensor suyo en todas las batallas que acometen . . .

Don't be simple, Sancho, replied don Quijote, and see this great Knight of the Red Cross was given by God to Spain as her patron and protector, especially in those difficult conflicts with the Moors that Spaniards have fought, thus they invoke and call upon him as their defender in all their battles . . .

(El) Sastre del Campillo, que cosía de balde y ponía el hilo— The tailor of Campillo, who sewed for nothing and even threw in the thread free; meaning: To work for the love of it.

(El) Secreto de Anchuelo, que lo supo todo el pueblo— The secret of Anchuelo, which all the village knew. This is a saying used to mock someone who, with great reservation, discloses something which is an open secret. Anchuelo is a town in the province of Madrid, and lies between two hills. The idiom is rooted in an old anecdote about a lovestruck shepherd and a young shepherdess from the region who would stand, one on each hill, and proclaim their amorous 'secrets' to each other.

Ser de Castellón de la Plana—Lit: To be from Castellón de la Plana; meaning: To be a flat-chested woman. The idiom is a play on the word *plana*, which means flat. Castellón de la Plana is a city in the Valencia region, eastern Spain.

Ser un Hércules/Sansón—To be a Hercules/Samson.

Si sale con barba, San Antón; si no, la Purísima Concepción— If it turns out to have a beard, St Anthony; if not, the Immaculate Conception. This is a saying used by someone carrying out a piece of work (i.e. a painting) with little conviction, or with little interest in the outcome. The expression is attributed to a second-rate painter, an imitator of Orbaneja.

Tal para cual, Pedro para Juan—This is used when speaking about two people to indicate that they are as bad as each other: Six of one half a dozen of the other. Same as: *Tal para cual, Pascuala con Pascual*.

Tan bueno es Pedro como su compañero—Pedro is as good as his companion; ironic saying meaning: Six of one, half a dozen of the other; They are as bad as each other.

Tanto monta, monta tanto, Isabel como Fernando—Tatamount/Equal to each other are Isabel and Fernando. Saying used to indicate that two people or things have the same value or standing. The expression was the motto of the Catholic Monarchs in the XV century, and appeared on all official documents and crests.

Tener más cojones que el caballo de Santiago—Lit: To have more balls than St. James' horse; meaning: To be very valiant/courageous. This refers to the fabled white horse that St James (patron of Spain) rode into battle against the Moors. (See also: *¡Santiago, y cierra, España!*, above)

Tener más moral que el Alcoyano—To have more enthusiasm/optimism/morale than Alcoyano; To keep going against all the odds. This alludes to a well-known, but third-rate, football team (and its enthusiastic supporters) from Alcoy in Alicante, renowned for their indomitable spirit.

Tener más paciencia que Job—To have the patience of Job.

(El) Tío Paco con la rebaja/ [Ya vendrá el tío Paco con la rebaja]—Uncle Paco with the reduction/ [Soon uncle Paco will come along with the reduction]. Meaning: That plans or projects frequently bear little resemblance to the end result, for such things are often dramatically changed and reduced in size/scope/content etc in the light of reality. Tío Paco is the proverbial personification of that which brings extravagant or exaggerated plans and dreams down to earth.

Topado ha Sancho con la horma de su zapato—Sancho has met the mould of his shoe [Similar to: *Dar con la horma de su zapato*—Lit: Meet the mould of one's shoe]. Meaning: To meet one's match; Also: To meet one's wishes.

(Las) Verdades de Perogrullo, [que a la mano cerrada llamaba puño]—Lit: The truths of Perogrullo, [who called a clenched hand a fist]; meaning: Self-evident truth; Truism. The fabled Perogrullo or Pero Grullo is thought to allude to a XIII century character who personified obvious truth, in contrast to Pedro Mentiras (Peter Lies). The name also appears on some official XIII century documents as the witness to the contracts or deeds in question.

Ver menos que Pepe Leches—Lit: To see less than Pepe Leches; meaning: To be short sighted.

¡Viva la Pepa!—Lit: Long live la Pepa. This is an exclamation used to denote a happy-go-lucky attitude to life, or devil-may-care irresponsibility. Though a little complicated for speakers of the English language (which does not use grammatical gender), the phrase originated in Cádiz when the Spanish Constitution of 1812 was proclaimed on 19 March—the feast of St José (Joseph). And since the word constitution (*constitución*) has a feminine gender in Spanish, and the feminine of José is Josefa (of which Pepa is the colloquial form), the idiom *¡Viva la Pepa!* was used at the time to mean Long live the Constitution!

Y salga el sol por Antequera—And let the sun rise over Antequera. Ironic phrase indicating the indifference of the speaker to the outcome/consequences of a particular matter or event. Another version is: *Salga el sol por Antequera y póngase por dondequiera*—Let the sun rise over Antequera and set wherever it likes. The saying is thought to have originated in the camp of the army of the Catholic Monarchs, during the conquest of Granada. The irony is manifested in the fact that Antequera lies to the west of Granada not to the east.

* * * *

2. THE USE OF KEY WORDS IN IDIOMS

As in other languages, Spanish also employs so-called key words as the building blocks which help form the basis of colloquial and slang expressions. Space does not permit us to include a comprehensive list here, but some examples of pivotal words in Spanish popular speech are given below.

ANDAR—TO WALK/TO GO

A literal translation is given along side each exclamation in sections A and B below to illustrate the colour and flavour of the original Spanish.

A. Examples of exclamations using *anda* to mean: **Get lost; Go to hell; Get stuffed**, etc.

¡Anda/Ve a freir espárragos!—Go fry asparagus!

¡Anda a pasear!—Go take a walk!

¡Anda a la mierda!—Go to the shit!

¡Anda y que te aguante tu abuela/tía!—Go and let your granny/aunt suffer you!

¡Anda y que te den morcilla!—Go, and may they give you blood sausage!

¡Anda y que te den un tiro/tres tiros!—Go, and may they shoot you once/three times!

¡Anda y que te folle un pez/un guarro!—Go, and may a fish/pig fuck you!

¡Anda y que te frían [un huevo]!—Go, and may they fry you [an egg]!

¡Anda y que te la casque tu madre!—Go, and may your mother crown you!

¡Anda y que te mate el Tato!—Go, and may *el Tato* kill you! (Antonio Sánchez, *El Tato*, was a well-known bull fighter)

¡Anda y que te ondulen!—Go, and may they undulate you!

¡Anda y que te pise una vaca!—Go, and may a cow trample you!

!Anda que te zurzan [con hilo negro]!—Go let them darn you [with black thread].

B. Exclamations meaning: **Damn, Good heavens, Bloody hell, Jeez,** etc:

¡Anda con Dios!—Go with God! (Also has literal meaning as a farewell phrase).
¡Anda la hostia!—Go the host!
¡Anda la leche!—Go the milk!
¡Anda la osa!—Go the bear!
¡Anda la puta!—Go the whore!
¡Anda ya!—Go now! Also: Get away [with you]; What a load of rubbish!

C. Miscellaneous expressions:

¡Anda con él/ella!—Lit: Go with him/her; meaning: I dare you!, Just you dare!
Andar a gatas—On all fours; To crawl.
Andar dando rodeo—Beat about the bush.
Andar de cabeza—Up to one's eyeballs/ears; Under pressure of work.
Andar/Bailar de coronilla—To work hard at it; To bend over backwards.
Andar por el/los suelo/s—To be at a low ebb; Rock bottom.
Andarse con pies de plomo—Act with caution/tact; Tread warily.
Andarse por las ramas—Beat about the bush.

D. Andalusian Expressions:

Andar a la brega—To slave away.
Andar a las duras y a las maduras—Through thick and thin.
Andar/Estar achuchado—To be in a difficult situation (usually monetarily).
Andar algo manga por hombro—To lack order or discipline.
Andar arañando—Not to waste a thing; Make use of everything down to the last crumb.
Andar como el caracol—To possess just the clothes on one's back/what you're standing up in.
Andar como las vacas del Tío Meleno—Not to follow any rules; To be a rule unto oneself.

Andar con el hato a cuestas —To be forever on the move.

Andar con siete/cien ojos—To be very cautious/wary.

Andar de cuca—To live it up; have a good time.

Andar en coplas/en boca/en lengua de la gente—To be the source of news or criticism; To be on everyone's lips.

Andar/Estar en el ajo—To be in the know.

Andar en haches y erres—To be involved in arguments/disputes.

Andar en palmas/palmitas—To be acclaimed.

Andar/Estar mal de la caja de cambios—To have a bad chest.

Andar/Estar mal de la chorla—To be crazy; A head case.

Andar suelto por ahí—To hang about the streets.

Andar trasteando—To rummage.

Andar uno a la que salta/salga—To be on the look out for any opportunity; Not to miss a trick.

Andar/Estar uno de capa caída—To be at a low ebb/in poor form.

CARA—FACE

Cara de alguacil/guardia civil—A harsh/severe face.

Cara de cemento [armado]—Brazen.

Cara de corcho—Cheeky; Brazen.

Cara de cuchillo—Hatchet face.

Cara de chiste—To look ridiculous.

Cara de hereje —An ugly face.

Cara de mala leche—A long/miserable/angry face.

Cara de monja boba—To look all innocent.

Cara de pan—A round face.

Cara de pascua(s)—A cheerful look/face; Look pleased.

Cara de pijo—To look silly/an idiot.

Cara de vinagre—Unfriendly/sour-faced look.

Cara o cruz—Heads or tails. To toss up for [something].

Dar cara a—To face up to.

Dar la cara—To face the consequences of one's actions.

Dar/Sacar la cara por—To stand up for [someone].

Echar a/en la cara—To reproach; Throw something in someone's face/teeth

Echar cara—To dare; To have a go/try.

Estar con cara de—To look like

Estar con la cara—To be broke/penniless; Not to have two pennies to rub together.

Guardar la cara—To hide; To avoid [someone/something].

Hacer cara a—To face; To stand up to.

Hacer la cara nueva—To smash [someone's] face in; ironic: To give [someone] a new face.

Lavar la cara a uno—To lick someone's boots.

Llenar la cara de aplausos/de dedos—To slap [someone's] face.

Partir/Romper la cara—To smash someone's face in.

Plantar cara a alguien—To confront someone; Stand up to someone.

Poner cara de circunstancias—To put on a sad face.

Poner cara de póquer—Poker faced [expression].

Poner cara de sargento—To wear a harsh expression.

Poner cara de viernes santo—To have a long/sad face.

Poner la cara del revés—To smash someone's face in.

Poner la cara como un mapa—To mark someone's face [with blows].

Sacar en cara—To throw in someone's face/teeth.

Tener cara—To be cheeky; To have a nerve.

Tener la cara como una paella—To have a spotty face.

Tener más cara que culo/espalda—To be cheekier than . . . / More brazen than; To have a nerve.

Tener más cara que un buey con flemones—Lit: To have a bigger face than an ox with an abscess; To have a real cheek/nerve.

Tener más cara que un elefante con paperas—Lit: To have a bigger face than an elephant with mumps; meaning: To be very cheeky.

Tener más cara que un saco de papas—Lit: To have a bigger face than a sack of potatoes; meaning: To be very cheeky.

Verse las caras—To have it out face to face.

CULO—ARSE

Con el culo al aire—In a difficult/embarrassing situation; Stranded.

Con el culo a rastras—To be in a fix/jam; To be on one's arse/beam ends.

Con el culo prieto—To be afraid; Scared to death.

Confundir el culo con las témporas—Not to know/tell one's arse from one's elbow.

Dar por culo—To screw someone.

Ir a tomar por culo—To go get stuffed/screwed.

Ir de culo/de puto culo—To be in difficulty; To go badly. Also: To be very busy; Up to one's ears in work.

Lamer el culo—To lick [someone's] arse; To brown-nose.

Limpiarse el culo con—To wipe one's arse with; meaning: Not to give a damn/shit about.

¡Métetelo en el culo!—Stick it up your arse!

Mojarse el culo—To get involved; To get one's feet wet.

Oír por el culo—To have cloth ears.

Pasárselo por el culo—Not to give a shit/about . . .

Pensar con el culo—To think with one's arse.

Poner el culo—To drop one's pants; To offer one's arse.

Romperse el culo—To work one's arse/butt off.

Tener/Ser un culo de mal asiento—To be a fidgety/restless person.

Tonto del culo—A complete idiot.

Traer de culo—To drive someone mad/round the bend.

Venir como zanahoria al culo—To be a perfect fit; a God-send.

Venir de culo—Ill-timed; Inopportune.

LECHE—MILK

A toda leche—Very fast.

Dar una leche—To hit/punch/thump someone.

Darse una leche—To come a cropper; To crash; Turn out badly.

De la leche—Bloody awful [e. g. Hace un tiempo de la leche— It's bloody awful weather]

Estar de mala leche—To be in a foul temper; To feel pissed off.

Echar leches—To go up the wall; To go wild/mad.

Haber muy mala leche—To be a lot of bad blood/ill-feeling (here, between them, etc.)

Ir a toda leche—To go very fast; To thunder along.

Ir/Salir echando/cagando leches—To go/leave in a hurry/very fast; To go like a bat out of hell; To go like the clappers.

¡La leche!—Bloody hell! Damn!

Leche—Vulgar expression for: semen; Spunk.

¡Leche!—Hell!

¡Leches!—No way! Get away!

Liarse a leches—To beat the hell out of each other.

Me cago en la leche—Shit! Damn!

¡Ni leche/s!—Nothing! Not a bloody thing!

¡Qué .... ni qué leche!—Rubbish/nonsense! My eye! My foot!

Pegarse una leche—To have an horrendous crash.

Poner a uno de mala leche—To annoy someone.

Ponerse de mala leche—To be in a foul mood.

¡Qué leches!—What the hell!

¡Qué leche tiene!—What a lucky/Jammy devil.

Ser la leche— To be annoying/a nuisance/a bore. [*¡Es la leche!*— It's such a pain. *Ese tío es la leche*—He/she is the pits/the end; also: He/she is fantastic/terrible/a bloody marvel.]

Ser una persona de mala leche—To be a nasty piece of work/an evil person.

Tener la leche avinagrada —To be bitter.

Tener mala leche—To be nasty, vindictive.

¡Una leche! —No way!

OJO—EYE

Costar un ojo de la cara—To cost an arm and a leg.

Mear en el ojo—Lit: To pee in the eye; meaning: To walk all over; To piss on.

Más seco que un ojo de tuerto—Lit: More dried up than the eye of a one-eyed man; meaning: Very thin/ Thin as a rake; also: In a dreadful situation.

¡No es nada lo del ojo!—There's more to it than meets the eye.

No pegar ojo en toda la noche—Not to sleep a wink all night.

¡Ojo!—Attention! Take care! Look out!

Ojo a la funerala/pava/virulé—A black eye

Ojo del culo—The anus.

Ojo morado—A black eye.

Saltar a los ojos—To be very obvious.

Ser el ojo derecho de—To be the apple of somebody's eye.

Tener a uno entre ojos—To dislike/loathe someone.

Ver con malos ojos—To look unfavourably on.

* * * *

3. UNIVERSAL THEMES

The following examples constitute a small selection of universal themes reflected in Spanish proverbs and idioms. The examples within each subject are not meant to be exhaustive, but have been chosen to illustrate the variety and richness of expression:

MONEY and POWER

Aconsejar no cuesta dinero—Advisers run no risks.

A la fea, el caudal de su padre la hermosea—The ugly woman, her father's fortune makes beautiful.

A poco dinero, poca salud—Poor in money, poor in health.

Al rico llamarle honrado, y al bueno llamarle necio—Call the rich man honest, and the good man an idiot.

(El) Ahorro es santo, porque hace milagros—Savings are saintly because they perform miracles.

Bien canta Marta cuando está harta—Martha sings well with her belly full.

Bien te quiero, bien te quiero; mas no te doy mi dinero—I love you, I love you; but you're not getting a penny. Refers to those who profess love and friendship, but when difficulties arise refuse to help.

Bienes mal adquiridos a nadie han enriquecido—Ill-gotten gains never thrive.

La buena vida es cara, la hay barata pero no es vida—The good life comes dear, it can be cheaper, but it isn't life.

(Las) Cuentas claras, y el chocolate espeso—Accounts clear and chocolate dark; meaning: Keep things [accounts] open and aboveboard.

Cuanto uno más tiene, más retiene—The more you have, the more you retain.

Dame dineros, y no consejos—Give me money, not advice.

De la mujer y el dinero no te burles, compañero—Don't mock women or money, dummy.

Dinero de suegro, dinero de pleito—Father-in-law's money, dispute/lawsuit money.

(El) Dinero es como los ratones, que oyendo ruido se esconde—Money is like mice, when it hears a noise it hides.

(El) Dinero es la causa de todos los males—Money is the root of all evil.

(El) Dinero lo cura todo—Money cures all ills.

(El) Dinero puede todo—Money is all-powerful; Money is power.

Dinero llama al dinero—Money begets money.

(El) Dinero no huele—Money has no smell.

(El) Dinero y la mujer, en la vejez son menester—Money and a woman, in old age are necessary.

Dineros son calidad—Money is quality.

Donde hay din, hay don—Where there's money, there's deference.

Donde el dinero hable, la lengua calle—Where money could talk, the tongue should be quiet.

Duros hacen blandos—Hard cash makes people weak.

El que pide prestado no tiene derecho a elegir—Beggars can't be choosers.

El que poco tiene, poco se precia—He who has little, boasts little.

En dinero y santidad, la mitad de la mitad—In money and in saintliness, half of the half.

Entre el honor y el dinero, lo segundo es lo primero—Between honour and money, the second is first.

Entre salud y dinero, salud quiero—Between health and money, I choose health.

Estar nadando en dinero—To be rolling in money.

Gastar dinero a mansalva/a manos llenas—To spend money like water.

Harto hay, pero está mal repartido—There's a surfeit [of money], but it's badly shared out.

(El) Hombre ruin, más ruin cuando más din—The miser: the more money the more miserly.

Lo barato sale caro—The cheap comes dear; The best is cheapest in the end.

Lo de balde es caro—The free comes dear; There's no such thing as a free lunch.

Mal suena el don sin el din—Don (deferential title) doesn't sound so good without dosh.

(El) Martillo de plata rompe las puertas de hierro—A silver hammer breaks down iron doors.

Más vale pan con amor, que gallina con dolor—It's better to eat dry bread in love than chicken in sorrow; Better a dinner of herbs than a stalled ox where hate is.

Nada proporciona fortuna como la misma fortuna—Nothing succeeds like success.

Ni prestes ni pidas prestado pues, a menudo, el préstamo desaparece con el amigo—Neither a borrower nor a lender be, for loan oft loses itself and friend.

No gastes más de lo que ganas—Don't live beyond your means.

No hay tal compañero como el dinero—Money is the best companion.

No pongas tu dinero en un jarro sin fondo—Don't send good money after bad.

No quiero, no quiero, pero echádmelo en el sombrero—No, no, but drop/throw it in the hat.

Nunca mucho costó poco, ni poco mucho—A lot never cost a little, nor a little a lot.

Para los bobos se hizo la mala fortuna—Bad luck was made for idiots.

Pobreza nunca alza cabeza—Poverty never gets off the ground.

Poderoso caballero es don dinero—A powerful lord is Mr Money.

Por dinero baila el perro, y por pan, si se lo dan—Lit: The dog dances for money and even for bread if offered; meaning: Things are usually done for profit rather than for altruistic motives.

Quien da su hacienda antes de la muerte, merece le den con un mazazo en la frente—Who disposes of his possessions before he dies, deserves to be hit on the head with a mallet.

Quien dinero tiene, alcanza lo que quiere—The rich achieve all they desire; Money is power.

Quien dinero tiene, come barato y sabio parece—The wealthy eat cheaply and appear wise.

Quien más tiene, más quiere—The more you have, the more you want.

Quien nada arriesga, nada gana—Nothing ventured, nothing gained.

Quien no se moja, no pasa el río—If you don't get your feet wet, you won't cross the river; meaning: Nothing ventured, nothing gained.

Quien poco tiene, poco puede—Little means, little able.

Quien tiene dineros, pinta panderos/tiene compañeros—Who has money, calls the shots/has friends.

Rey es el amor, y el dinero, emperador—Love is a king, but money is an emperor.

Si eres amo de tu dinero, bueno; pero si tu dinero es tu amo, malo—If you are the master of your money, good, but if your money is your master, bad.

Si te dan dinero, tómalo al punto; si te lo piden, cambia de asunto—If offered money, take in straight away; if asked for money, change the subject.

Sólo los ricos tienen crédito—Only the rich can borrow money/get credit.

Tanto mata lo mucho como lo poco—In for a penny, in for a pound; Might as well get hanged for a sheep as a lamb.

Vivir al tenor de los que tienen más dinero que tú—To keep up with the Joneses.

GOD AND FATE

God:

Al erizo, feo y todo, Dios lo hizo—We are all God's creatures.

Al que Dios no le da hijos, el diablo le da sobrinos—Lit: To those whom God does not grant children, the devil grants nephews/nieces; meaning: To be left with the responsibility of others.

¡Anda con Dios!—God be with you! Also: My God!

A la buena de Dios—Any old how.

Armar la de Dios/Armar la de Dios es Cristo—Lit: To cause that of God/that of God is Christ; meaning: To raise hell/ cause a tremendous fuss.

Barriga llena, a Dios alaba—A full stomach praises God.

Como Dios—Fantastic, Superb (Trabajar como Dios—Indicates an outstanding performance).

Como Dios manda—As it should be; The way it/one is supposed to.

Como Dios pintó a Perico—Effortless; A piece of cake; A cinch.

Como que hay un Dios—As sure as eggs is eggs.

Con Dios—Good-bye.

Costar/Necesitar Dios y su ayuda—To take/To need a lot of work/help.

De los amigos me guarde Dios, que de los enemigos me guardo yo—God deliver me from my friends, from mine enemies I'll deliver myself.

Dios los cría y ellos se juntan—Birds of a feather flock together.

Dios nos crió hermanos, pero no primos—To be nobody's fool; Not to be taken for a ride.

Más que Dios—Much; A lot.

Más vale dirigirse a Dios que a los santos—Better go straight to the top.

Ni Dios—Nobody; Not even God.

Ni Dios que lo fundó—No way! Absolutely not.

No hay Dios que ... —Nobody.

¡Que Dios nos coja confesados!—God/The Lord help us!

¡Que venga/baje Dios y lo vea!—I'll eat my hat. Also in Andalusia: As God is my witness.

Rediez/Rediós—Good God!

Ser un contradiós—To be a sin.

Todo Dios—Absolutely everybody.

God/Fate Decrees:

A ira de Dios no hay cosa fuerte—There's no overcoming God's anger.

A quien Dios quiere bien, la casa le sabe—Whom God loves well, his house is well blest.

A quien Dios quiere, la perra le pare lechones—Lit: Whom God loves well, his dog will have a litter of piglets; meaning: One's luck depends on God.

Acá y allá, Dios dirá—Down here or up there, God ordains.

Cada uno estornuda como Dios le ayuda—Each person's sneeze is as God decrees.

Cuando Dios no quiere, los santos no pueden—When God does not want to [do/grant something], the Saints can't [are powerless].

Cuando Dios quiere, con todos aires llueve—Lit: When God wills, it rains with any wind; meaning: everything is subject to God's will.

Cuna/Matrimonio y mortaja, del cielo bajan—Lit: Cradle/ Marriage and shroud, from heaven come down; meaning: All things of this world are ordained by fate/heaven/God.

Estar de Dios—Meant to be; To be fated.

(El) Hombre propone, y Dios dispone—Man proposes, and God disposes.

Más vale a quien Dios ayuda, que quien mucho madruga—It's better to have God on your side than be an early riser.

Nadie se muere hasta que Dios quiere—You'll die when your number's up (when God wills it) and not before.

Nunca viene sino lo que Dios quiere—God/Fate decrees the course of things.

Human beings must do their bit:

A Dios rogando y con el mazo dando—God helps them that help themselves.

A quien no habla, no le oye Dios—If you don't speak up, you won't be heard.

A quien se ayuda, Dios le ayuda—As above.

Al que madruga, Dios le ayuda—The early bird catches the worm.

Quien se guarda, Dios le guarda—God helps them that help themselves.

Quien se muda, Dios le ayuda—God helps those that mend their ways.

God/Fate—Fairness:

Dios aprieta pero no ahoga—God squeezes but does not strangle; meaning: Don't give up hope, God will help in the end. These things are sent to try us.

Dios da el frío conforme la ropa—Lit: God sends the cold according to the clothes; meaning: God provides the means to meet the difficulty; God makes the backs for the burden.

Dios, que da la llaga, da la medicina—God sends the illness, but also the remedy.

God/Fate—Unfairness:

Dios da pan/almendras a quien no tiene dientes/muelas—God sends bread/almonds to those who have no teeth; It's a cruel/an unfair world.

Dios da mocos al que no tiene pañuelo—Lit: God gives a snotty nose to those who have no handkerchief; As above.

Díome Dios un huevo, y diómelo huero—God sent me an egg, and sent it rotten. Phrase also used to criticize people who are always lamenting their bad luck, or who say that the little they have is useless.

CHRIST

A Cristo prendieron en el huerto porque allí se estuvo quieto—Lit: They caught Christ in the garden [of Gethsemane] because he stood still there (accepted his fate). Ironic saying, indicating that the speaker will not take things lying down.

A la Virgen, salves; a los Cristos, credos; pero los cuartos, quedos—To the Virgin, Hail Marys; to Christs, Creeds; but quarters [old Spanish coin], I keep. Phrase used to criticize those who spend much time at prayer but who are uncharitable/tight-fisted.

A mal Cristo, mucha sangre—For a bad Christ, much blood; meaning: The sensational hides poor workmanship (often refers to cheap works of art or literature).

Armar un [la de un] Cristo—To kick up/create a fuss.

Con el Cristo en la boca—With one's heart in one's mouth.

¡Cristo que lo fundó!—Don't you believe it!

Cristo y la madre—Everyone and his brother/ The world and his wife.

Como a un santo Cristo un par de pistolas—Phrase indicating incongruence: It's like dungarees on a queen. Also: To look awful on someone; Not to suit someone at all. (Same as: Como a un santo/cura un par de pistolas).

Como el pie de Cristo/Como los pies de un santo—As hard as the foot of Christ/the feet of a saint. As hard as wood; As tough as nails.

(El) Cristo al río—Into the river with Christ! No-one will stop me!

Donde Cristo dio las tres voces/perdió el gorro/la alpargata—Lit: Where Christ called out thrice/lost his cap/his sandal; meaning: In the middle of nowhere, in the back of beyond; out in the sticks.

Echar los cristos a rodar—Lit: To set/let off Christs; meaning: To display a violent temper [in order to get one's way].

Hasta verte Cristo mío—Down the hatch! Bottoms up!

Ir hecho un Cristo/Ponerse como un Cristo—To get/To be absolutely filthy (or in a real mess).

No hay Cristo que lo entienda—Absolutely nobody understands it.

Ni Cristo pasó de la cruz, ni yo paso de aquí—Christ didn't move from the cross, and I'm not moving from here. Phrase indicating wilful intransigence.

Ni por un Cristo—Not for the world.

Poner/Dejarle a uno como un Cristo/Ecce Homo—To call someone every name under the sun.

Recristo—Good God! Jesus Christ!

Sacar el Cristo—To try to bully or badger into (doing something).

Todo Cristo—Absolutely everyone.

THE RELIGIOUS AND THE PROFANE

Acabar como el rosario de la aurora—Lit:To end like the dawn rosary; meaning:To end in a fight/brawl.

A chico santo, medio padrenuestro; a gran santo, echar el resto—For a second class saint, half an Our Father, for a great saint, the whole thing.

A santo que no me agrada, ni padrenuestro ni nada—To a saint I don't like [I offer] neither an Our Father nor anything else.

A un santo, rézale tanto y más cuanto; pero a una santa con media Avemaría basta—To a male saint pray a lot and more; but to a female saint half an Ave Maria will do.

Al que es un alma de Dios, lo engañan tós—A child of God is cheated/taken for a ride by all.

Alzarse/Cargar con el santo y la limosna—Lit: To make off with the saint and the alms; meaning:To make off with the whole caboodle/lot; Make a clean sweep.

Amigo de Santo Tomás, siempre tomas y nunca das—Lit: Friend of St Thomas, always take and never give; meaning: a mean person; tight-fisted.

Amor de monja y fuego de estopa y viento de culo, todo es uno.—The love of a nun and fire of hemp and wind from the arse: it's all the same.

Amor de monja y pedo de fraile, todo es aire.—A nun's love and a friar's fart: it's all air.

¿A Santo de qué? —For heaven's/goodness sake;Why on earth.

Donde San Pedro perdió el gorro—Lit: Where St Peter lost his cap; meaning: In the middle of nowhere; In the back of beyond; Out in the sticks.

Beber el caliz—To drink the chalice [of sorrow].

Also: *Caliz de amargura/dolor*—Cup of bitterness/sorrow.

Caga el rey, caga el Papa; sin cagar, nadie se escapa—Lit:The king shits, the Pope shits, nobody escapes without shitting; meaning:We're all human and have human needs.

Cagar hostias—To go very fast.

Comehostias—Lit: a host eater; meaning: a pious person.

Comerse los santos—To be very pious/devout.

Como dijo Herodes, ¡te jodes!—As Herod said: fuck off!

Como puta en cuaresma—Lit: Like a whore during Lent; meaning: Not earning much money;To go hungry.

Como San Jinojo en el cielo—Ignored by all.

Como una patena—Lit: Like a paten; meaning: very clean.

Limpio/reluciente como una patena—As clean as a new pin; Spick-and-span.

Desnudar un santo para vestir otro—To rob Peter to pay Paul.

Echar los kiries—To throw up kyries; meaning: To vomit (Alludes to the prayer kyrie eleison (Lord have mercy) said in mass.

El que no nada, se ahoga [y flota al tercer día]—He who doesn't swim, drowns [and floats on the third day]; meaning: Sink or swim.

En la casa del cura, siempre jartura—In the priest's house there's always a surfeit [of food].

En menos que canta el gallo—In less time than the cock crows; Quickly.

En menos que se santigua/persigna un cura loco—In less time than it takes a mad priest to make the sign of the cross; Quickly.

Estar como unas pascuas—To be as happy as a sandboy.

Estar en Belén—To be day dreaming; Up in the clouds.

Estar en misa y repicando/en el plato y en las tajadas—ironic: You can't do two things at the same time.

Estar hecho la [santa] Pascua/la santísima mierda—To feel like the most holy shit.

Hacer el viacrucis—Lit: To do the stations of the cross; meaning: To go to bars; To go on a pub crawl.

Hacer la pascua a uno—To do the dirty on someone; To make it difficult for someone.

Hacerle comulgar a uno con ruedas de molino—To be gullible.

Hablar en cristiano—To talk in plain language/Spanish.

Hay una Salomé que me ha quitado la cabeza/el sentido—There's a Salome who has driven me out of my mind.

¡Hostias en vinagre!—Lit: Hosts in vinegar/pickled hosts; meaning: No way!

¡Hostia puta/divina!—Lit: Whore/Divine host; meaning: Good heavens! Gosh! etc.

Irse el santo al cielo—To forget what one is doing/about to say; To be day-dreaming/ miles away.

Lo que el diablo se ha de llevar, llevémonoslo nosotros—Better grab [it] before someone else does.

Llegar a Belén—Lit: To arrive at Bethlehem/at the nativity crib; meaning: To arrive home drunk on Christmas day.

Llegar y besar al santo—To pull it off at the first attempt.

Llorar como una magdalena—Cry like a baby; Cry one's eyes out.

Mear agua bendita—Lit: To pee holy water; meaning: To be very religious.

Meter/Poner el dedo en la llaga—To hit a raw nerve; Put one's finger on a sore spot.

Meterse en belenes—To get into a jam/fix.

(La) Misa del gallo—Midnight mass.

(La) Misa, dígala el cura—It's somebody else's responsibility; It not my/your business.

Nacer con el santo de espaldas—To be born unlucky.

No cantar el kirieleisón—Lit: Not to sing kyrie eleison; meaning: Not to be ruled by anyone; Not to toe the line.

No saber de la misa la media/la mitad—Not to know the first thing about.

No saber a qué santo encomendarse—Not to know which way to turn.

No ser santo de su devoción—To be no favourite of; Not the be very keen on.

No vale lo que costó bautizarle/el pan que come—Worthless.

O todos moros, o todos cristianos—What's sauce for the goose, is sauce for the gander.

Parece que le ha hecho la boca de un fraile—Always asking for things.

Pasar las de Caín—To go through hell.

Pegar/Dar una hostia—Lit: To hit/give a host; meaning: To give/be asking for a punch/smack.

Poner a uno como un santo—To give someone a good telling off.

Por mí, que diga misa—Lit: For me, they can say mass; meaning: As far as I'm concerned, I don't give a damn.

Quedarse para vestir santos/un santo—To be left on the shelf.

Rata de sacristía—Very pious woman.

Relumbra más que una hostia/el copón/el Corpus—As clean/bright as a new pin; Spick-and-span.

Saber como el avemaría—To know something backwards.

Santa Rita, Santa Rita, lo que se da, no se quita—Once you give something, you can't take it back.

Santas Pascuas—It can't be helped; So be it.

Santo y seña—Password; Slogan.

Ser [devoto] de la virgen del puño—Lit: To be devoted to the Virgin of the fist; meaning: To be mean/tight-fisted.

Ser más papista/católico que el Papa—To out-Herod Herod.

Ser más puta que Santa Rita—To be a bigger whore than St Rita.

Ser un calvario/un inri—To be a cross/a heavy burden.

Also: *Pasar un calvario*—To suffer agonies.

Ser un contradiós—To be a sin.

Ser un pedazo de carne bautizada—A dim-witted person.

Si en el sexto no hay remisoria, ¿quién es el guapo que va a la gloria?—If for breaking the 6th [commandment] there's no remission, who is the lucky one that will reach heaven?

(La) Siesta del cura/del carnero—To doze off/take a nap in mid-morning.

Tener el santo de cara—To have great luck.

Tener el santo de espaldas—To do nothing right; Everything is going wrong.

Tener un belén—To have an illicit affair.

Traer por la calle de la amargura—To drive someone mad; To make someone's life hell.

Visitar los sagrarios—Lit: To visit the tabernacles; meaning: To go to bars; Go on a pub crawl.

Volvérsele a uno el santo de espaldas—One's luck has changed for the worse.

HUMOUR

Slang expressions in Spanish are particularly graphic and earthy. Many employ the macabre imagery of black humour, with its often politically incorrect depictions; so-called *humor marrón*, with its scatalogical or lavatorial allusions; and picaresque wit, tinged with both Sanchopanzist ingenuousness and a hint of healthy irony. The selection below reflects many of these elements.

Agarrar una pulmonía celeste—To catch a celestial pneumonia.

¡Anda que pareces una hormiga paralítica!—Come on, you're like a paralytic ant; meaning: Very slow.

Cargar con el santo/el muerto—To carry the saint/corpse; meaning: To carry the can; Take the blame for.

Cargale/Echarle a uno el muerto—Throw someone the corpse; meaning: To pin something on someone; Also: To pass the buck.

Comemierdas—A shit eater; A contemptible person.

¡Cómprate ....—Expressions meaning: **Get lost; buzz/push off; Stop bothering me; Give it a rest,** etc:

 ¡Cómprate un bosque y piérdete! —Lit: Buy yourself a wood/forest and lose yourself in it!

 ¡Cómprate un calvo y péinalo!—Lit: Buy yourself a bald man and comb his hair!

 ¡Cómprate un desierto y bárrelo!—Lit: Buy yourself a desert and sweep it!

 ¡Cómprate un muerto y llórale!—Lit: Buy yourself a corpse a cry over it!

De pura mierda —By an almighty fluke; By chance.

Enrollarse más que una persiana—More rolled-up than a blind; To be heavy going; long winded.

Eramos pocos, y parió la abuela—Ironic saying, Lit: There were few enough of us and grandmother gave birth; meaning: That's all we needed! As if we didn't have enough problems!

Estar de puta madre—Lit: To be a mother whore; meaning: Fantastic; Outstanding.

Gastar menos que un ruso en catecismo—To spend less than a Russian in catechism; meaning: To be mean/stingy.

Hablar por los codos—To talk through your elbows; meaning: To be a chatterbox.

¡Mal . . . !—Used in expressions to mean: **Drop dead! Go to hell!**:

¡Mal chinche te pique!—May a bad bug bite you!

¡Mal rayo te parta!—May a bad ray strike you!

¡Mal toro te coja!—May a bad bull get you!

¡Mal tiro te den/peguen!—May a bad shot hit you!

Mandar a la mierda—To send to hell.

Más agarrado que el chotis—Lit: As tightly held as a *chotis* [traditional dance of Madrid]; meaning: Very mean/tight-fisted; A scrooge.

Más basto que . . .—Expressions meaning: **Coarser than; More uncouth than**, etc.

Más basto que la Bernarda que se bajaba las bragas a pedos—Coarser than Bernarda who pulled her pants down farting.

Más basto que pegarle a un padre con un calcetín sudado—More uncouth than hitting your father with a sweaty sock.

Más basto que un bocadillo de hostias—Coarser than a host sandwich.

Más basto que un rosario de melones—Coarser than a rosary of melons.

Más basto que unas bragas de esparto—Coarser than a pair of esparto grass knickers.

Más basto que unos sostenes de hojalata—Coarser than tinplate bra/brassiere.

Más chupado que la pipa de un indio—Lit: Sucked more than an Indian's pipe; meaning: Very easy; easy as pie; a cinch; also: Very thin; as thin as a rake.

Más difícil que cagar a pulso/de pie/p'arriba—More difficult than shitting standing up.

Más duro que la pata de mi abuela [que sólo queda el hueso]—Harder than my grandmother's leg [only the bone remains]; meaning: Hard as nails; Tough as old boots.

Más feo que . . . — Uglier than . . .

el diablo—the devil

el no tener—having nothing

morderse las uñas—biting one's nails

pegar a su padre—hitting one's father

un dolor de muelas—a toothache

una cucaracha—a cockroach

Más lento que ... —Slower than ...

    el caballo del malo—the baddy's horse (in cowboy films).

    un desfile de cojos—a parade of cripples

    una hormiga paralítica—a paralytic ant.

Más liado que la pata de un romano—More tied-up than a Roman's leg; meaning: A lot of problems/work/trouble, etc.

Más listo que el hambre—Lit: As smart as hunger; meaning: As smart as they come.

Más negro que ... —Blacker than ...

    el alma de Judas—Judas's soul

    el sobaco de un ciego—a blindman's arm pit

    la muerte—death

Más pesado que dormir un cerdo/una vaca en brazos—Heavier than cradling a pig/cow in one's arms.

Más tira moza que soga—A young woman pulls more than a rope.

Más tonto que ... —More stupid than ...

    hacerle la permanente a un calvo—giving a bald man a perm.

    hacerle una paja a un muerto—wanking a corpse.

Me cago en ... —I shit on ... : meaning: **Shit! Damn! Bloody Hell! Jeez!**, etc:

    la leche [que mamaste]—the milk [that you suckled]

    la madre que te parió—the mother who bore you

    la puta—the whore

    tus muertos—your dead [relatives]

Mear en el ojo—Lit: To pee in the eye; meaning: To walk all over; To piss on.

Mear en la boca—Lit: To pee in the mouth; meaning: To flatten, crush.

Mear torcido—Lit: To pee crooked, meaning: Turn out badly; To make a mess of something.

Mearse de risa/de gusto—To pee oneself with laughter/pleasure.

(La) Mierda, cuanto más la hurgan/se revuelve, más hiede/huele—The more you stir shit, the more it smells.

Mierda que no ahoga, engorda—Shit that does not kill, fattens; meaning: saying that mocks the scrupulously clean or excessively hygienic.

Mierda veo, mierda quiero —Lit: I see shit, I want shit; meaning: Capricious.

Mierdecilla—A little shit; A nobody; Insignificant.

Mierdica—A coward.

Mierdoso—Filthy.

(El) Muerto al hoyo, y el vivo, al bollo—The dead man to the hole, and the living to the bread roll.

No comerse/conseguir una mierda—Not to get a thing; Come away empty handed.

No hay amor verdadero, hasta el primer pedo camero—True love is proved with the first fart in bed.

No tener donde caerse muerto—To have nowhere to drop down dead; meaning: To be broke; Not to have two pennies to rub together.

No valer una mierda—Worthless.

Para cuatro días que vivimos y dos hace nublado—Life only lasts four days, and two of those are cloudy.

Para el tiempo que he de estar en este convento, cágome dentro—Lit: For the time I have to spend in the convent, I'll shit inside; meaning: I couldn't care less; It does not affect me; It's of no importance to me.

Parecer un entierro de tercera—Lit: To look like a third class funeral; meaning: To look so bored.

Pillar meando—To catch someone peeing; To surprise someone.

Ser un vivalavirgen—Lit; To be a long-live-the virgin; meaning: Someone with a devil-may-care, irresponsible attitude.

Si tu mujer quiere que te eches de un tejado abajo, pídele a Dios que sea bajo—If your wife asks you to throw yourself off the roof, pray it's a low building.

> Also: *Si tu mujer te pide que te tires por la ventana, pídele a Dios que sea de un primer piso*—If your wife asks you to throw yourself out of the window, pray it's on the first floor.

(La) Suerte del enano que fue a cagar, y se cagó en la mano—Lit: The luck of the dwarf who went to shit, and shat on his hand; A real disaster.

(La) Suerte de la fea, la bonita la desea—The luck of the ugly woman, the beauty desires it; meaning: usually refers to luck in marriage, i.e. that an ugly woman who has a pleasant disposition is often more fortunate.

> Similar to: *Fea con gracia, mejor que guapa*—Better an ugly woman with charm than a beauty.

*Tonto de ... *—Lit: As stupid as/as thick as/ as silly as ...

> *el carajo/la picha/la polla*—a prick
> *los cojones/los huevos*—balls.

Tu madre será una santa, pero tú eres un hijo de puta—Your mother may be a saint, but you're a son of a bitch.

Una mujer hermosa es un peligro; una mujer fea, un peligro y una desgracia—A beautiful woman is a danger; an ugly woman a danger and a misfortune.

Unos nacen con una estrella y otros estrellados—Lit: Some are born under a [lucky] star, others seeing stars; meaning: Fate/Fortune smiles on some but not on others.

* * * *

4. SAYINGS USED BY OLD WOMEN BY THE FIRE

The following is a selection of the 750 proverbs and idioms compiled by Iñigo López de Mendoza, Marquis of Santillana, in his XV century work: *Refranes que dizen las viejas tras el huego* (sic).

A buen bocado, buen grito.—Lit: To a good bite, a good scream; meaning: The result of too much good food is painful illness.

A buen callar llaman Sancho. [Also in *Corbacho, Guzmán de Alfarache, Quijote, Criticón.*] —Sage Silence is Sancho's name; meaning: advises moderation and discretion in speech.

A buen entendedor, pocas palabras. [*Zifar, Celestina, Guzmán de Alfarache, Quijote.*]—A word to the wise.

A buey viejo no cates abrigo.—Don't teach your grandmother to suck eggs.

A caballo comedor, cabestro corto.—Lit: For a greedy horse, a short rein; meaning: A dissolute person should be kept under control.

A casas viejas, puertas nuevas.—Lit: Old houses, new doors; meaning: Mutton dressed as lamb.

A chica cama, échate en medio.—Lit: On a small bed, lie in the middle; meaning: Make the best of a bad job.

A do pensáis que hay tocinos, no hay estacas. [*Quijote.*]—Lit: Where you expect to find bacon, there are no hooks; meaning: counsels caution in one's estimation of other people, especially those who give the impression of being rich.

A do te quieren mucho, no vayas a menudo. [*Buen Amor.*]— Friendships should not be abused.

A esotra puerta que esta no te abre. [*Lazarillo.*]—Try another door, this one will not open to you.

A la vejez, aladares de pez.—Lit: In old age, gills of a fish; meaning: proverb used to mock elderly men who dyed their hair so as to appear younger.
Similar to: *A la vejez, viruelas.*—In old age, chickenpox.

A mal abad, mal monacillo.—To a bad abbot, a bad altar boy.

A mal capellán, mal sacristán.—To a bad chaplain, a worse sacristan.

A mal hecho, ruego y pecho. [*Buen Amor.*]—After a bad deed, supplication and courage.

A mengua de pan, buenas son tortas.—Lacking bread, crackers/cakes will do nicely.

A mengua de carne, buenos son pollos con tocino.—Lacking red meat, chicken and fatty bacon will do nicely.

A otro perro con ese hueso.—Pull the other one; Go tell it to the marines.

A pan duro, diente agudo.—Stale/hard bread, a sharp tooth.

A perro viejo, tus, tus. [*Celestina.*]—A wise man is not easily deceived.

A quien dan no escoge. [*Buen Amor.*]—Beggars can't be choosers.

A quien Dios quiere bien, la casa le sabe. [*Quijote.*]—Whom God loves well, his house is well blest.

A río vuelto, ganancia de pescadores. [*Celestina.*]—Lit: A turbulent river is the fisherman's gain; meaning: Much profit may be reaped from confusion.

A todo hay maña, sino a la muerte. [*Quijote.*]—There's a remedy for everything except death.

(El) Abad donde canta, dende yanta. [*Celestina, Quijote.*]—
The abbot eats where he sings for his meat.

Al hombre por la palabra, y al buey por el cuerno.—Lit: A man
by his word, an ox by his horn; meaning: A man's word is his
bond.

Al gran salto, gran quebranto.—The higher one rises, the
harder one falls.

Allá van leyes, do quieren reyes. [*Quijote, Criticón.*]—There are
no rules for the rich and powerful.

Allégate a los buenos, serás uno de ellos. [*Quijote.*]—Keep the
company of respectable people and you will become one of
them.

Allí se mete como piojo en costura.—Like sardines in a can.

Amor de niño, agua en cesto.—A child's love is fleeting.

*Amor de monja y fuego de estopa y viento de culo, todo es
uno.*—The love of a nun and fire of hemp and wind from
the arse: it all the same.

Antes de mil años, todos seremos canos.—Eat, drink and be
merry, for tomorrow we die.

*Antes que cases, cata qué haces, que no es nudo que así
desates.*—Before you marry, watch what you are doing, for
the knot is not easily undone; meaning: Look before you
leap.

Asna con pollino, no va derecha al molino.—The lovesick
cannot be relied upon to perform their work properly.

Asno de muchos, lobos lo comen. [*Buen Amor, Criticón.*]—Lit:
The mule/ass of many, is devoured by wolves; meaning:
Shared responsibility means unaccountability.

Beata con devoción, las tocas bajas y el rabo ladrón.—A Pious woman with devotion [has] a long headdress and a thief's tail.

Becerrilla mansa, mama a su madre y a la ajena. [*Celestina, Guzmán de Alfarache.*]—Lit: A docile calf, suckles from its own mother and others; meaning: A pleasant person is well received by all.

Bien ama quien nunca olvida.—He who truly loves never forgets.

Bien canta Marta cuando está harta. [*Criticón.*]—Martha sings well on a full stomach; [reminiscent of the saying: An army marches on its stomach.]

Bien sabe el asno en cuya casa rebuzna.—Familiarity breeds contempt.

(El) Bien suena, y el mal vuela.—Lit: Good sounds, evil flies; meaning: News of bad deeds travels faster than good; Bad news travels fast.

Bocado de mal pan, no lo comas ni lo des a tu can.—Lit: A bite of rotten bread, neither eat it yourself nor feed it to your dog.

Buen amigo es el gato, sino que rasguña.—A cat is a good friend, but it can scratch.

Buen esfuerzo quebranta mala ventura. [*Zifar, Buen Amor, Quijote.*]—A stout heart breaks bad luck.

Buenas son mangas después de Pascua. [*Celestina, Guzmán de Alfarache, Quijote, Criticón.*] —Late gifts are just as welcome.

Caballo que alcanza, pasar querrá.—We always desire more than we achieve.

Cabra va por viña, cual madre, tal hija.—A chip off the old block; Like mother, like daughter.

Cada gallo, en su muladar.—Every cock will crow upon its own dunghill.

Cada uno con su ventura.—To each his own fortune.

Cada uno dice de la feria como le va en ella. [*Celestina, Criticón.*]—Lit: Each person speaks of the fair according to how it went for him; meaning: Speak as you find.

Callen barbas y hablen cartas. [*Quijote.*]—Lit: Let writing speak and beards be silent; meaning: Show written proof, for words are of little value.

Can con rabia, a su dueño muerde.—Lit: A rabid dog will bite his master; meaning: Fury holds no respect.

Cantar mal y porfiar. [*Criticón.*]—Brazen and unabashed.

Cantarillo que muchas veces va a la fuente, o deja el asa o la frente. [*Zifar, Quijote.*]—Lit: The pitcher that goes often to the spring/well, either leaves its handle or its lip behind; meaning: Don't push your luck too far.

Castígame mi madre, y yo trómpogelas. [*Quijote.*]—The more my mother beats me, the more I whip the top.

Codicia mala, saco rompe. [*Guzmán de Alfarache, Quijote.*]— Avarice bursts the sack; meaning: Covet all, lose all.

Comer uva y cagar racimo.—Eat grapes and shit bunches.

¿Cómo te hiciste calvo? Pelo a pelo pelando. [*Corbacho.*]—Lit: How did you become bald? Hair by hair cutting; meaning: Little strokes fell great oaks.

Cría el cuervo, sacarte ha el ojo.—Breed a crow and it will pick your eyes out; meaning: To bite the hand that feeds you.

Cuando el villano está rico, ni tiene pariente ni amigo.
[*Celestina.*]—When the humble go up in the world, they
have neither family nor friends.

Cuando te dieren la vaquilla, acorre con la soguilla. [*Corbacho, Buen Amor, Quijote.*]—When they give you a calf,
make haste with the halter.

De compadre a compadre, chinche en el ojo.—Beware of false
friends.

De hombre heredado no te verás vengado.—You can't get
revenge on a well-rooted man.

De hora a hora, Dios mejora.—Put your trust in God.

*Del río manso me guarde Dios, que del fuerte yo me
guardaré.*—God deliver me from my friends, from mine
enemies I'll deliver myself. Also: Still waters run deep.

Derramadora de la harina, allegadora de la ceniza. [*Corbacho.*]—Lit: Spiller of flour, collector of ashes; meaning:
refers to person who takes great care with things of little
value, but neglects those of greater importance. Penny wise
and pound foolish.

Dime con quién andabas y decirte he qué hablabas. [*Quijote.*]—Lit: Tell me with whom you were walking, and I'll tell
you about what you were talking.
Similar to: *Díme con quién andas, te diré quién eres.*)
Meaning: A man is known by the company he keeps.

Dijo el asno al mulo: tira allá, orejudo.—The ass said to the
mule: move out of the way big ears; meaning: The pot calling
the kettle black.

Dijo la sartén a la caldera: tírate allá culinegra.—Lit: As the
frying pan said to the kettle: move out of the way black-
bottom; meaning: The pot calling the kettle black.

Dio Dios habas a quien no tiene quijadas. [*Celestina.*]—God gave beans to those who have no jaw [to chew them].

Dios me dé contienda con quien me entienda. [*Criticón.*]—May God send me quarrels with people I can reason with.

Dueña que mucho mira, poco hila.—The mistress who spends her time looking out of the window, doesn't do much spinning.

Duerme con tu enemigo, y no con tu vecino.—Sleep with your enemy, not with your neighbour.

Duerme quien duerme, y no duerme quien algo debe.—Lit: He sleeps who sleeps, and not he who is in debt; meaning: An honourable person sleeps less easily when in debt than when in pain.

Echa la piedra y esconde la mano.—Lit: Throw the stone and conceal your hand; meaning: refers to people who stir up trouble then shelter/recoil from the consequences.

Echate a enfermar, verás quién te quiere bien o quién te quiere mal.—Become ill, you'll discover who your friends are.

En boca cerrada no entra mosca.—Lit: In a closed mouth no fly enters; meaning: If you keep your mouth shut, you won't put your foot in it.

En burlas ni en veras, con tu señor no partas peras. [*Criticón.*]—Lit: Neither in jest nor in earnest should you ever cut pears with your master; meaning: Avoid familiarity with superiors.

En cada tierra, su uso. [*Guzmán de Alfarache, Quijote.*]—In each country, its customs; meaning: When in Rome, do as the Romans do.

En casa del herrero, cuchillo mangorrero.—Lit: In the blacksmith's house, a poor knife; meaning: The shoemaker's son/wife always goes barefoot; There's none worse shod than the shoemaker's wife.

En casa del mezquino, más manda la mujer que el marido.—In a weak man's house, the wife wears the trousers.

En casa llena, aína se hace cena. [*Celestina.*]—In a well-stocked house the supper is soon cooked.

En la aldehuela, más mal hay que suena. [*Celestina, Quijote.*]—In the village, there's more amiss than meets the eye.

En luengo camino y en cama angosta se conocen los amigos.—On a long journey and in a narrow bed one knows one's friends.

En manos está el pandero de quien lo sabrá tañer. [*Celestina, Quijote.*]—Lit: The tambourine is in the hands of the one who knows how to play it; meaning: The person who knows the job is the one most likely to bring it to a successful conclusion.

Erguido como gallo en cortijo.—Arrogant/vain as a cock in a farmyard.

Gato maullador, nunca buen cazador.—Lit: A meowing cat, never a good hunter; meaning: He/she is all talk; A lot of words, but little action.

Grano a grano, hinche la gallina el papo. —Lit: Grain by grain, the hen inflates its crop; meaning: little by little.

Hallado ha Sancho su rocín.—Sancho has found his nag; meaning: refers to two people who are inseparable. Similar to: *Allá va Sancho con su rocín.*

Haré, haré; más vale un "toma" que dos "te daré". [*Quijote.*]—One gift is worth two promises.

Haz bien y no cates a quién. [*Zifar, Criticón.*]—Do good and don't think for whom.

Holgar, gallinas, que muerto es el gallo.—Hens, be of good cheer, the cock is dead; meaning: While the cat's away the mice will play.

Hombre apercibido, medio combatido. [*Celestina, Quijote.*]— Forewarned is forearmed.

Hombre harto no es comedor.—Overindulgence kills appetite.

Hombres con frío y cochinos hacen gran ruido.—People who suffer cold, and pigs, make a lot of noise.

Honra sin provecho, anillo en el dedo. [*Celestina.*]—Lit: Honour/reputation without benefit, a ring on the finger; meaning: warns against spending on things that only feed vanity.

Huésped que se convida, ligero es de hartar.—An uninvited guest is quickly satisfied; meaning: Don't look a gift horse in the mouth.

Jo, que te estriego. [*Celestina, Quijote.*]—Whoa, let me scrub you!; meaning: used to dismiss words of praise; Fine words butter no parsnips!

Justicia, mas no por nuestra casa. [*Criticón.*]—Punishment yes, but not for us.

Ládreme el perro, y no me muerda.—A barking dog never bites.

Lo que en la leche se mama, en la mortaja sale.—Lit: What's suckled in the milk, will come out in the shroud; meaning: What's bred in the bone will come out in the flesh.

Madrastra, el nombre le abasta.—Stepmother, the very name says it all.

Mal Lara uses a similar saying: *La madrasta no es buena ni en cera ni en pasta.*—A stepmother is bad whether of wax or sugarpaste. Similar to: *Madrasta, aun de azúcar amarga*—A stepmother, even one made of sugar, is bitter.

Mal de muchos, gozo es. [*Zifar, Corbacho.*]—The misfortune of many is a joy.

Manos duchas comen truchas.—Skillful/experienced hands eat trout; meaning: Skill/dexterity is the mother of good results.

Maravillóse la muerte de la degollada. [*Quijote.*]—The dead woman was afraid of the one with her throat slit.

Más da el duro que el desnudo. [*Criticón.*]—The hard man gives more than the naked.

Más cerca tengo mis dientes que mis parientes. [*Criticón.*]—Lit: My teeth are closer to me than my family; meaning: Look after number one/yourself first.

Más sabe el loco en su casa que el cuerdo en la ajena. [*Corbacho, Quijote, Criticón.*]—The madman knows more in his own house than the sane man in another's; meaning: Better results are achieved if you stay within your own environment.

Más vale con mal asno contender, que la leña a cuestas traer. [*Buen Amor.*]—It's better to contend with a doltish mule, than to carry the wood on your back

Más vale pájaro en mano que buitre volando. [*Guzmán de Alfarache, Quijote.*]—Lit: Better a bird in the hand than a vulture in flight; meaning: A bird in the hand is worth two in the bush.

Más vale quien Dios ayuda que quien mucho madruga. [*Celestina, Quijote.*]—It's better to have God on your side than be an early riser.

Más vale salto de mata, que ruego de hombres buenos. [*Qui-jote.*]—A leap over the hedge is better than good men's prayers.

Más vale tuerto que ciego.—One eye is better than none.

Más vale vergüenza en cara que mancilla en corazón. [*Buen Amor.*]—Better to face up to a difficult situation than shy away and regret it later.
Similar to: *Más vale ponerse una vez colorado que ciento amarillo/morado.*—Better to turn red once than a hundred times yellow/purple.

Mucho hablar, mucho errar. [*Buen Amor.*]—He who talks too much, errs exceedingly.

Muchos son los amigos y pocos los escogidos. [*Guzmán de Alfarache.*]—Lit: Many are friends, but few are chosen.
Similar to: *Muchos son los llamados y pocos los escogidos.*—Many are called, but few are chosen.

Mudar costumbre, par es de muerte. [*Celestina.*]—Old habits die hard.

Muera gata y muera harta. [*Quijote.*]—Let the cat die with its belly full.

Muera Sansón y cuantos con él son. [*Corbacho, Guzmán de Alfarache, Quijote.*]—Lit: Let Samson die and all those with him; meaning: The time for valour has arrived.

(La) Mujer y la gallina, por andar se pierden aína. [*Qui-jote.*]—Roaming causes women and hens to get lost; meaning: cautions that women [and hens] should not stray far from home.
Similar to: *La mujer y la gallina, hasta la casa de la vecina.*—Women and hens [should not go further than] the neighbour's house.

Nadar, nadar, y a la orilla ahogar.—Lit: Swim, swim only to die at the shore; meaning: To lose something at the last moment.

Ni más pechar ni más medrar.—Neither too much endeavour/ work, nor too much prosperity [is good for you].

Ni mozo mocoso, ni potro sarnoso.—Neither a snivelling lad, nor a mangy colt.

No con quien naces, sino con quien paces. [*Guzmán de Alfarache, Quijote.*]—Not with whom you were bred, but with whom you have fed; A man is known by the company he keeps.

No digas quién eres, que tú te lo dirás.—Don't bother saying who you are, you'll only be telling yourself; It's not necessary to say who you are, it will soon become apparent.

No fíes ni porfíes.—Neither guileless nor stubborn be; Neither trusting nor importunate be.

No hay bien conocido hasta que es perdido. [*Guzmán de Alfarache.*]—You don't know the value of a good thing until you've lost it.

No hay espada sin vuelta, ni puta sin alcahueta.—There's no sword without a scabbard, nor whore without a procuress.

No hay peor burla que la verdadera.—There's no worse joke/jest/jibe than the truth; meaning: cautions against making a person's defects the butt of one's jokes.

No hay peor sordo que el que no quiere oír. [*Criticón.*]— There's nobody deafer than one who doesn't want to hear.

No son todos hombres los que mean a la pared.—They are not all men who pee against the wall; meaning: cautions that one should not judge things by external signs or appearances.

Nuestro gozo en el pozo. [*Celestina.*]—Lit: Our enjoyment down the well; meaning: That's the end of all our illusions.

O rico, o pinjado.—[Return] rich or hanged.

Obras son querencias. [*Criticón.*]—Deeds are love; Love is works not words. (Ac: Obras son amores, que no buenas razones.)

Ojos que no ven, corazón que no quiebra. [*Quijote.*]—What the eye doesn't see, the heart doesn't grieve for.

Oro es lo que oro vale.—Gold is what has gold's worth; meaning: The real value of things is not what they are worth in money.

Oveja que bala, bocado pierde.—The sheep that bleats, misses the bite; meaning: cautions against becoming distracted from one's main objective.

Palabras y plumas el viento las lleva.—Words and feathers, the wind blows them away; cautions not to trust in airy promises.

(El) Pan comido, la compañía deshecha. [*Quijote.*]—Lit: [Once the] bread is eaten, the friendship is terminated; meaning: refers to people who end friendships once they have served their usefulness.

Para cada puerco hay su Sanmartín.—Lit: St. Martin's day comes for every pig; meaning: Everyone gets their comeuppance/just deserts in the end.

Parto malo, e hija en cabo. [*Criticón.*]—A bad/painful birth, and on top of it a girl child: meaning: To achieve poor results after so much hard work.
  Also: *Llevar mala noche y parir hija.*—Have a bad night, and give birth to a girl.

Pensar no es saber.—Thinking is not knowing.

Peor es lo roto que lo descosido.—A tear is worse than a split seam.

(El) Perro del hortelano, ni come las berzas, ni las deja comer. [*Lope de Vega.*]—Lit: The gardener's dog neither eats cabbage nor lets others eat it; meaning: A dog in a manger.

Piensan los enamorados que los otros tienen los ojos que-
brados. [*Criticón.*]—Lovers think that other people are blind.

(La) Pobreza es escalera del infierno.—Poverty is the
ladder/staircase to hell.

Pon tu hacienda en concejo: uno hace blanco, otro bermejo.
[*Quijote.*]—Put your state [of affairs] to public scrutiny:
some will say it's white, others black [lit: *bermejo*—red].

Por el dinero baila el perro [y por pan si se lo dan].—Lit: The
dog dances for money [and even for bread if offered];
meaning: things are usually done not for altruistic motives
but for profit.

Quien al cielo escupe, en su cara le cae.—Spit at the sky/
heaven, and it falls back in your face; cautions against arrogance, for you will reap the consequences.

Quien bien quiere a Beltrán, bien quiere a su can. [*Celestina.*]—
Lit: Who love Beltran, well loves his dog; meaning: Love me,
love my dog.

Quien bien te hará, o se te irá, o se te morirá. [*Criticón.*]—
Who is good to you will eventually either leave you or die;
meaning: the unfortunate always lose their benefactors.

*Quien bien tiene y mal escoge, por mal que le venga no se
enoje.*—One who has something good and rejects it for
something bad, should not grumble about the misfortune
that results.

Quien burla al burlador cien días gana de perdón. [*Celestina.*]
—Who mocks the mocker gains a hundred days pardon.
Similar to: *Quien roba a un ladrón, tiene cien años de
perdón.*—Who steal from a thief, earns a hundred years
forgiveness.

*Quien da lo suyo antes de su muerte, merece que le den con
un mazazo en la frente.*—Who disposes of his possessions
before he dies, deserves to be hit on the head with a mallet.

Quien de locura enferma, tarde sana [o nunca]. [*Zifar.*]—He who becomes mad, recovers late [or never]; cautions that little can be expected of people of poor judgment.

Quien destaja, no baraja. [*Quijote.*]—He who cuts [the cards], doesn't shuffle [them]; advises against doing two different things at the same time.

Quien dinero tiene, alcanza lo que quiere.—The rich achieve all they desire; Money is power.

Quien lengua ha, a Roma va. [*Criticón.*]—With a tongue in your head, you can reach any destination.

Quien malos pasos anda, malos polvos levanta.—False/bad steps lead to bad consequences.

Quien no habla, no le oye Dios.—If you don't speak, you won't be heard.

Quien no sabe de abuelo, no sabe de bueno. [*Criticón.*]—If you don't know [the love of] a grandfather, you don't know what is good.

(El) Rey va do puede y no do quiere.—The king goes where he can and not where he wants.

Si me viste, burléme; si no me viste, calléme. [*Celestina.*]—If you saw me, I joke; if you didn't see me, I keep quiet. Refers to thieves who if caught in the act try to laugh it off as a joke, and if not caught they simply keep quiet.

Si se perdieron los anillos, aquí quedaron los dedillos.—Lit: If you lost your rings, you kept your fingers; meaning: cautions against regretting the loss of incidentals when what is of most importance remains.

Si te vi, no me acuerdo.—Lit: If I saw you, I don't remember. Refers to the contempt with which the ungrateful respond to favours rendered.

Sobre cuernos, penitencia.—Lit: On top of horns [being cuck-olded], penitence; meaning: Sinned against and blamed for it.

Tan bueno es Pedro como su asno.—Lit: Pedro is as good as his mule; meaning: Neither one is to be trusted.

(La) Tierra que me sé, por madre me la he. [*Guzmán de Alfarache*]—The land where I was reared, I hold as my mother.
Similar to: *La tierra do me criare, démela Dios por madre.*—The land where I was reared, may God make it my mother.

Todos los duelos con pan son buenos. [*Guzmán de Alfarache, Quijote.*]—Suffering/problems are more easily borne when one has sufficient means/funds.

Tornaos a vuestro menester, que zapatero solíades ser. [*Guzmán de Alfarache.*]—Every man to his trade.

Una alma sola, ni canta ni llora. [*Buen Amor, Celestina.*]—A single soul neither sings nor weeps.

Una golondrina no hace verano. [*Celestina, Quijote.*]—One swallow doesn't make a summer.

(La) Una mano lava a la otra, y las dos al rostro. [*Guzmán de Alfarache.*]—One hand washes the other, and both wash the face.

Uno muere de atafea, y otro la desea.—One dies of surfeit/satiety, the other of desire/lack.

Uso hace maestro.—Practice makes perfect.

(La) Verdad es hija de Dios.—Truth is God's child.

Vióse el perro en bragas de cerro [y no conoció a su com-pañero]. [*Corbacho, Quijote.*]—Look there at the dog in a doublet!; meaning: cautions that a person who has gone up in the world often does not want to recognise former companions.

Viva la gallina con su pepita. [*Celestina, Quijote.*]—Let the hen live with her pip (disease of fowls); meaning: Often the cure is worse than the illness.

Notes

All translations into English of Spanish proverbs and quotations are by J. & S. Serrano

1. Mal Lara, J. de, *Philosophia Vulgar*, Sevilla, 1568, *Préambulo IX, A quantas cosas aprovecha la sciencia de los refranes*.
   Translation of quotation:
   Los refranes ... Son como piedras preciosas salteadas por las ropas de gran precio, que arrebatan los ojos con sus lumbres y la disposición da a los oyentes gran contento y, como son de notar, quédanse en la memoria.
2. Mann Phillips, M., *The Adages of Erasmus*, Cambridge University Press, 1964, p. 199.
3. Cervantes Saavedra, M. de, *El Ingenioso Hidalgo Don Quijote de la Mancha*, Madrid: Ediciones Castilla, 1947, Book I, ch.21, p.163.
4. *ibid.*, in poem: *Del Donoso Poeta Entre verado a Sancho Panza y Rocinante*, Prólogo, p. 14.
5. Rojas, F. de, *La Celestina*, ed. B. M. Damiani, Madrid: Cátedra, 1982, Act XV, p.256.
6. *Lazarillo de Tormes*, in *La novela picaresca española*, vol.I, ed. F. Rico, Barcelona: Planeta, 1967, p.35.
7. Swift, J., *The Polite Conversation*, ed. H. Davis, Oxford, 1939-68; Introduction.

8. Clemencín, D., in Cervantes *op. cit.*, Comentarios, p.1177.

9. Feijóo, B.J., *Falibilidad de los adagios*, from *Cartas eruditas,* vol.III, in *Obras escogidas*, ed. V. de la Fuente, (Biblioteca de Autores Españoles), Madrid: Atlas, 1952, p.552.

10. Mann Phillips, M., *op. cit.*, p.27.

11. Feijóo, B. J., *op. cit.*, p. 553.

12. *ibid.*, p. 555.

13. Cervantes Saavedra, M. de, *op.cit.*, Book II, ch.10, p. 530.

14. Plato, *Protagoras*, trans. W.K.C. Guthrie, Reading: Penguin Books, 1983, p.77, (342).

15. *loc. cit.*, (343).

16. *loc. cit.*

17. Mann Phillips, M., *op. cit.*, p.5.

18. *ibid.* p.xiii.

19. *ibid.* p.171.

20. Ruiz, J. (Arcipreste de Hita), *El Libro de Buen Amor*, ed. J. Ducamin, Toulouse: Privat, 1901. vv.169–70.

21. Casares, J., *Introducción de la Lexicografía moderna*, Madrid: CSIC, 1969, p.192.

22. Sánchez, J.M., Prologue in Santillana: *Refranes que dicen las viejas tras el fuego*, Madrid, 1910, p.11.

23. Mir, M., in Introduction to Correas: *Vocabulario de refranes y frases proverbiales y otras fórmulas comunes de la lengua castellana*, Madrid, 1924, p.xiii.

24. López de Mendoza, I. (Marqués de Santillana), Address to Principe de Castilla, Don Enrique IV in *Proverbios Utilísimos del Ilustre Caballero D. Iñigo López de Mendoza, Marqués de Santillana, glosados por el Doctor Pero Díaz de Toledo*, Madrid, 1787.

25. Mann Phillips, M, *op. cit.*, p.172.

26. Montoto y Rautenstrauch, L., *Consejo de un maestro Antonio Machado y Alvarez, "Demófilo"*, in *Por Aquellas Calendas. Vida y milagros del magnífico caballero Don Nadie*, Madrid: Renacimiento, 1930.

27. Unamuno, Miguel de, *Del sentimiento trágico de la vida, Obras Completas*, vol. VII, Madrid: Escelicer, 1966, p.291.

28. Unamuno, Miguel de, *Ganivet, filósofo*, in *Nuevos Ensayos, op.cit*, vol. III, p.1091.

29. Unamuno, Miguel de, *Del sentimiento trágico de la vida*, in *op.cit.*, vol. VII, p.293.

30. Calderón de la Barca, P., *El gran teatro del mundo*, Scene II, in *Autos Sacramentales*, vol. I, Madrid: Espasa-Calpe, 1984.

31. Quoted in W.J. Oates, *The Stoic and Epicurean Philosophers*, New York: Random House, 1940, p.225.

32. Unamuno, Miguel de, *El porvenir de España,* in *op.cit.* vol.III, p.643.

33. *Lazarillo de Tormes*, in *La novela picaresca española*, vol.I, ed. F. Rico, Barcelona: Planeta, 1967, p.31.

34. Torrente Ballester, G., cited in Manuel Barrios: *Repertorio de modismos andaluces*, Universidad de Cádiz, l991, p.7.

35. Castro, A., *El pensamiento de Cervantes*, Barcelona: Noguer, 1972, p.184.

36. Mal Lara, J. de, *op. cit.*, Sevilla, 1568, *Preámbulos, Del origen de la philosophia vulgar*.

37. This proverb was used by the Golden-Age writer Felipe Godínez (1588–1639?) as the title of one of his plays.

38. For an in-depth discussion of the influence of Erasmus on Spanish thought see: Bataillon, M., *Erasme et l'Espagne*, 3 vols., compiled by D. Devoto, edited by C. Amiel, Geneve: Droz, 1991.

39. Mal Lara, J. de, *op. cit.*, *Preámbulo VI: De la qualidad de los refranes que se tratan*.

40. Fernán Caballero, (Cecilia Böhl de Faber), *Refranes y máximas populares recogidos en los pueblos del campo*, (Biblioteca de Autores Españoles, CXL), Madrid: Atlas, 1961, pp.257–276.

41. Alatorre, M. F., *Refranes cantados y proverbializados*, in *Nueva Revista de Filología Hispánica*, XV, Méjico, 1961, p.168.

42. Jeremiah VIII, v.23, Can the Ethiopian change his skin? or the leopard his spots?

Selected Bibliography

Alarcos LLorach, E., *La lengua de los Proverbios Morales de Don Sem Tob*, in *Revista de Filología Española*, XXXV, Madrid, 1951, pp. 248–308.

Alatorre, M. F., *Refranes cantados y proverbializados*, in *Nueva Revista de Filología Hispánica*, XV, Méjico, 1961, pp. 155–168.

Alemán, M., *Guzmán de Alfarache* (1604), ed. S. Gili Gaya, 5 vols., Madrid: La Lectura, 1926–36.

Arguijo, J. de, *Colección de Cuentos* (1605), in *Sales españolas*, ed. A. Paz y Meliá, Madrid, 1902, pp. 91–210.

Barriobero y Herrán, E., *Los viejos Cuentos españoles. Elegidos en las colecciones de Arguijo, Garibay, Pinedo y el Duque de Frías,* Madrid: Mundo Latino, 1930.

Barrios, M., *Repertorio de modismos andaluces*, Universidad Cádiz, 1991.

Beinhauer, W., *El español coloquial*, Madrid: Gredos, 1985.

Bernal Rodríguez, M., *El hábito no hace al monje. Clero y pueblo en los refraneros españoles del Siglo de Oro,* Sevilla: Padilla Libros Editores, 1994.

Campo, J. G. and Barella, A., *Diccionario de Refranes*, Madrid: Espasa-Calpe, 1993.

Cantos populares españoles, ed. F. Rodríguez Marín, 5 vols., Sevilla: F. Alvarez y Compañía, 1882–83; Madrid: Atlas, 1951.

Caro Baroja, J. M., *Ensayo sobre la Cultura Popular española*, Madrid: Editorial Dosbe, 1979.

Cela, C.J., *Diccionario secreto*, 2 vols., Madrid-Barcelona: Alfaguara, 1968–71.

Cejador, J., *Refranero castellano*, 3 vols., Madrid: Sucesores de Hernando, 1928–29.

Cervantes Saavedra, M. de, *El Ingenioso Hidalgo Don Quijote de la Mancha*, Madrid: Ediciones Castilla, 1947.

Correas, G., *Vocabulario de refranes y frases proverbiales y otras fórmulas comunes de la lengua castellana* (1627), ed. M. Mir., Madrid, 1924.

Covarrubias Orozco, S. de, *Tesoro de la lengua castellana o española, según la impresión de 1611, con las adiciones de Benito Remigio Noydens publicadas en la de 1674,* ed. M. de Riquer, Barcelona: Horta, 1943; Madrid, 1979.

Cuentos castellanos de tradición oral, ed. J. Díaz, Valladolid: Ambito, 1985.

Cuentos viejos de la vieja España, Del siglo XIII al XVIII, ed. F. C. Sainz de Robles, Madrid: Aguilar, 1957.

Delicado, F., *Retrato de la lozana andaluza* (1528), ed. J. del Val, Madrid: Taurus, 1980.

Escobar, Fray Luis de, *Quinientos proverbios de consejos y avisos, en forma de letanía*, in J. M. Sbarbi, *El Refranero General Español*, vol. VII, Madrid: Imp. A. Gómez Fuentenebro, 1874–76, 1980.

Espinosa, F., *Refranero*, ed. E. S. O'Kane, in *Boletín de la Real Academia Española,* anejo XVIII, Madrid, 1967.

Fernán Caballero, (Cecilia Böhl de Faber), *Cuentos y poesías populares andaluces,* Revista Mercantil, Sevilla, 1859.

Fernán Caballero, (Cecilia Böhl de Faber), *Refranes y máximas populares recogidos en los pueblos del campo*, (Biblioteca de Autores Españoles, CXL), Madrid: Atlas, 1961.

Góngora y Argote, L. de, *Obras poéticas*, ed. R. Foulché-Delbosc, 3 vols, New York: The Hispanic Society, 1921.

Gracián, B., *El Criticón*, ed. M. Romera-Navarro, 3 vols., University of Pennsylvania Press, 1938.

Horozco, S. de, *Teatro Universal de Proverbios*, ed. J. L. Alonso Hernández, Universidad de Salamanca, 1986.

Iribarren, J. M., *El porqué de los dichos*, Madrid: Aguilar, 1955, 1996.

Junceda, L., *Diccionario de refranes*, (Prologue by G. Torrente Ballester), Madrid: Espasa-Calpe, 1996.

Lazarillo de Tormes (1554), in *La novela picaresca española*, vol.I, ed. F. Rico, Barcelona: Planeta, 1967.

El Libro del cauallero Zifar (c. 1300), ed. C. P. Wagner, University of Michigan, 1929.

Lope de Vega, *Obras escogidas,* ed. F. C. Sainz de Robles, 3 vols., Madrid: Aguilar, 1946-55.

López de Mendoza, I. (Marqués de Santillana), *Proverbios de Gloriosa Doctrina e Frustuosa Enseñança de Iñigo López de Mendoza, según el Códice N.J. 13 de El Escorial,* ed. J. Rogerio Sánchez, Madrid: Librería General de Victoriano Suárez, 1928.

López de Mendoza, I. (Marqués de Santillana), *Refranes que dicen las viejas tras el fuego* (1508), ed. U. Cronan in *Revue Hispanique*, XXV, Paris, 1991.

Machado Alvarez, A., *Modismos populares* in *Estudios sobre literatura popular*, (Biblioteca de las Tradiciones Populares Españolas, V), Sevilla, 1884, pp. 27-89.

Machado Alvarez, A. and Castro, F., *Cuentos, leyendas y costumbres populares*, Sevilla, 1872.

Mal Lara, J. de, *Philosophia Vulgar. Primera parte que contiene mil refranes glosados*, Sevilla, 1568.

Martínez de Toledo, A., *Arcipreste de Talavera o Corbacho*, ed. M. Gerli, Madrid: Cátedra, 1992.

Martínez Kleiser, L., *Refranero general ideológico español*, Madrid: Real Academia Española, 1953; 1989.

Montoto y Rautenstrauch, L., *Personajes, personas y personillas que corren por las tierras de ambas Castillas*, 3 vols., Sevilla: El Correo de Andalucía, 1911-13.

Nuñez, Hernán, *Refranes o Proverbios en romance, que nuevamente colligió y glossó el Comendador Hernán Núñez. Van puestos por la orden del Abc...* , Salamanca: Cánoua, 1555.

O'Kane, E. S., *Refranes y frases proverbiales españolas de la Edad Media*, in *Boletín de la Real Academia Española*, anejo I, Madrid, 1959.

Pérez Galdós, B., *Episodios Nacionales*, in *Obras completas*, vols. I,II, & III, ed. F. C. Sainz de Robles, 6 vols., Madrid: Aguilar, 1941, 1971.

Pinto Crespo, V., *Inquisición y control ideológico en la España del siglo XVI*, Madrid: Taurus, 1983.

Quevedo, F. de, *Obras completas,* ed. L. Astrana Marín, 2 vols., Madrid: Aguilar, 1942.

Real Academia Española, *Diccionario de Autoridades*, 6 vols., Madrid, 1726–1739.

Real Academia Española, *Diccionario de la lengua española,* 1st to 21st eds., Madrid, 1780–1992.

Refranero español. Colección de ocho mil refranes populares, ed. J. Bergua, Madrid: Clásicos Bergua, 1936, 1976.

Rodríguez Marín, F., *Más de 21.000 refranes castellanos no contenidos en la copiosa colección del Maestro Gonzalo Correas*, Madrid: Imp. de la Revista de Archivos, 1926.

Rodríguez Marín, F., *Todavía 10.700 refranes más no registrados por el Maestro Correas,* Madrid, 1941.

Rojas, F. de, *La Celestina*, ed. B.M. Damiani, Madrid: Cátedra, 1982.

Romancea proverbiorum (c.1350), ed. J. Rius Serra, in *Revista de Filología Española*, XIII, Madrid, 1926, pp. 364-372.

Romancero, ed. G. Di Stefano, Madrid: Clásicos Taurus, 1993.

Ruiz, J., (Arcipreste de Hita), *El Libro de Buen Amor*, ed. J. Ducamin, Toulouse: Privat, 1901.

Samaniego, F. M. de, *Fábulas en verso castellano*, 2 vols., Madrid: Ibarra, 1781–84.

Santa Cruz, M. de, *Floresta española de apotegmas*, 1574, (Sociedad de Bibliófilos Españoles, XXIX), Madrid, 1953.

Sbarbi, J. M., *Gran Diccionario de Refranes de la Lengua Española,* ed. M.J. García, Buenos Aires: Editorial Joaquín Gil, 1943.

Sbarbi, J. M., *El Refranero General Español*, 10 vols., Imp. de A. Gómez Fuentenebro, Madrid, 1874–76; 1980.

Sem Tob, *Proverbios morales*, ed. E. González Lanuza, Buenos Aires: Sociedad Hebráica Argentina, 1958.

Timoneda, J. de, *El Sobremesa y alivio de caminantes* (1569), ed. B.C. Aribau, (Biblioteca de Autores Españoles, III), Madrid, 1846, pp. 169–183.

Valdés, J. de, *Diálogo de la lengua*, ed. J. F. Montesinos, Madrid: Clásicos Castellanos, 1928.

Vallés, P., *Libro de Refranes compilado por el orden del ABC, en el qual se contienen quatro mil y trezientos refranes* (Zaragoza, 1549), ed. M. García, Madrid, 1917.

Vergara y Martín, G. M., *Cantares, refranes, adagios . . . referentes a curas, monjas, frailes y sacristanes*, Madrid: Sucesores de Hernando, 1929.

Vergara y Martín, G. M., *Mil cantares populares amorosos*, Madrid: Sucesores de Hernando, 1921.

SPANISH VERBS: SER AND ESTAR
Juan and Susan Serrano
> *"This book will make a handy reference tool for teachers. It is the type of text that should be included in university bookstores for purchase by serious students of Spanish. In advanced classes where the difficult nuances of the Spanish language are taught, this would be an excellent choice for an indepth study of ser and estar."*
> —**The Modern Language Journal**

An invaluable aid for professors of Spanish! Here is the definitive key to mastering the Spanish verbs SER and ESTAR. Eight chapters, with a number of sub-headings for easy reference, take the beginning to advanced student through the subtleties and nuances of the two "to be" verbs. Dozens of lively dialogues are included to reinforce appropriate usage.
220 pages • 5 1/2 x 8 1/2 • 0-7818-0024-2 • W • $8.95pb • (292)

Bilingual Spanish-interest books

DICTIONARY OF 1,000 SPANISH PROVERBS
edited by Peter Mertvago
Organized alphabetically by key word, each Spanish proverb is presented with its English translation for quick reference. A distinction is drawn between proverbs that are identical to their English language counterparts and ones that are equivalent translations (providing students with the meaning of the proverb instead of a literal translation).
131 pages • 5 1/2 x 8 1/2 • bilingual • 0-7818-0412-4 • W • $11.95pb • (254)

TREASURY OF SPANISH LOVE POEMS, QUOTATIONS & PROVERBS
edited by Juan and Susan Serrano
This charming bilingual gift edition is also an enticing learning tool for Spanish at its best. It is a collection of popular Spanish love poems, quotations and proverbs, spanning eight centuries, in the original Spanish with side-by-side English translation. Among the poets included are de la Vega, Calderon and Garcia Marquez. A companion audiocassette, in which the works are read by native Spanish speakers and English-speaking actors, is available for students who want to work on pronunciation and speaking skills.
128 pages • 5 x 7 • 0-7818-0358-6 • W • $11.95 hardcover • (589)
2 cassettes (approx. 2 hours) • 0-7818-0365-9 • W • $12.95 • (584)

TREASURY OF CLASSIC SPANISH LOVE SHORT STORIES IN SPANISH AND ENGLISH
edited by Bonnie May
Here is a wonderful classroom aid for students of Spanish language or literature. Included are the following 5 short stories by classic Spanish literary masters: "The Abencerraje and Fair Xarifa" by Jorge de Montemayor; "The Wedding of Camacho" by Miguel de Cervantes Saavedra; "The Moonbeam" by Gustavo Adolfo Bécquer; "Dream Story" by Emilia Pardo Bazán; and "A Story of Love" by Miguel de Unamuno. Each story is presented in the original Spanish with side-by-side English translation on the facing page.
157 pages • 5 x 7 • 0-7818-0512-0 • W • $11.95hc • (604)

Spanish Dictionaries

SPANISH-ENGLISH/ENGLISH-SPANISH PRACTICAL DICTIONARY
Arthur Swift Butterfield
· includes over 35,000 entries
· a phonetic guide to pronunciation in both languages
· handy glossary of menu terms
· a bilingual list of irregular verbs
· a bilingual list of abbreviations
407 pages • 5 ¾ x8 ¼ • 35,000 entries •0-7818-0179-6 NA • $9.95pb •(211)

SPANISH-ENGLISH/ENGLISH-SPANISH *CONCISE* DICTIONARY (Latin American)
Ila Warner
· 8,000 entries
· Contains the distinct vocabulary found throughout the Caribbean and Central and South America
· phonetic pronunciation in both languages
· includes a list of cuisines from Spanish speaking countries
310 pages • 4 x 6 • 8,000 entries • 0-7818-0261-X • W • $11.95pb • (258)

also available in a handy pocket size:
SPANISH-ENGLISH/ENGLISH-SPANISH *COMPACT* DICTIONARY
310 pages • 3 ½ x 4 ¾ • 8,000 entries • 0-7818-0497-3 • W • $8.95pb • (549)

SPANISH-ENGLISH/ENGLISH-SPANISH DICTIONARY OF COMPUTER TERMS
Alfredo U. Chiri

With over 8,000 entries, the Spanish-English/English-Spanish Dictionary of Computer Terms will prove an invaluable reference books for students, travelers, and business people. The terms are accurately translated from English to Spanish and vice versa. The Spanish translation represents the actual computer jargon and corresponds to the actual English computer jargon. Phonetics follow every word in both the Spanish and English sections, making the book "user-friendly" for all.

212 pages • 5 1/2 x 8 1/2 • 8,000 entries • 0-7818-0148-6 • W • $16.95 hardcover • (36)

Spanish Language Guides

500 REALLY USEFUL SPANISH WORDS AND PHRASES FOR CHILDREN
Carol Watson and Janet de Saulles
Illustrated by Shelagh McNicholas

Now children ages 7-10 learning Spanish have this delightfully illustrated guide to help them along. This book presents words and vocabulary builders in categories like "Meeting People," "Finding the Way," "Eating Out," and "Games and Sports" among others. Each illustrated full-color page presents words and situations in English, and then provides the Spanish words with pronunciation.

32 pages • 8 x 10 1/4 • full-color illus. • 0-7818-0262-8 USA • $8.95hc • (17)

SPANISH GRAMMAR
Twenty-one lessons provide the student with a firm grasp of the spoken language and the basic vocabulary needed to communicate in Spanish, both on the American continent and in Europe. The lessons begin with basics like "The Alphabet," "Parts of Speech," and "The Spanish Sentence" and move on to topics such as "Reflexive Verbs," Grammatical concepts are explained in detail and drills, prose passages, and vocabulary are provided for practice.

211 pages • 5 1/2 x 8 1/2 • 0-87052-893-9 • W • $12.95pb • (273)

MASTERING SPANISH, book and audiocassettes
& MASTERING ADVANCED SPANISH,
book and audio cassettes
by Robert Clark

This two-part series offers reliable, reasonably priced contemporary language guides. The Mastering Series' method of instruction combines a full length text with lively dialogues, essential vocabulary, and important grammar exercises. Each text contains 20 situational lessons, including topics such as traveling by train, dining out, asking for directions, etc. The books are complete instruction guides integrated with audiotapes, read by native Spanish speakers, which teach correct pronunciation without repetition. Each book may be bought separately or together with the audiocassettes. *Mastering Spanish* was originally published by Macmillan of London and has been successfully tested throughout the world. It is a proven teaching method which allows students to gain a strong grasp of the language and excellent pronunciation and grammar skills.

MASTERING SPANISH:
322 pages • 5 1/2 x 8 1/2 • 0-87052-059-8 USA • $11.95 • (527)
2 Cassettes: • 0-87052-067-9 USA • $12.95 • (528)
MASTERING ADVANCED SPANISH:
326 pages • 5 1/2 x 8 1/2 • 0-7818-0081-1 • W • $14.95pb • (413)
2 Cassettes: • 0-7818-0089-7 • W • $12.95 • (426)

Prices subject to change without notice. To purchase Hippocrene Books contact your local bookstore, call (718) 454 2366, or write to: HIPPOCRENE BOOKS, 171 Madison Avenue, New York, NY 10016. Please enclose check or money order, adding $5.00 shipping (UPS) for the first book and $.50 for each additional book.